I love Patty Bourne! When I met her 15 or so years ago, I was drawn to her zest for life, her easy humor, and her unabashed candor. Through the years of our ensuing friendship, like magnets we are pulled together over and over…most often to mull ideas about teaching with "art and heart."

Inside the Music Classroom captures the zest, humor, and candor of Patty's presence and places them on the page right in front of us. Her words talk to us; they guide us through her special brand of homespun wisdom for 'growing' children and for loving music teaching.

Having successful experiences with folks both tall (university teacher preparation) and small (elementary classroom music) gives Patty an especially astute standing place from which to let us peer inside her music class. Books for elementary classroom and music teachers that offer activities, sequences, resources, and connections to theoretical frameworks are plentiful. Very few, however, are steeped with a spirit for grounding and enriching the lives of teachers and students, as this book is. This book has a wealth of principles and practices that can inspire and guide any new or seasoned teacher. I love Patty Bourne's book!

—*Dr. Peggy D. Bennett*
Professor of Music Education, Oberlin Conservatory of Music
Director of the MusicPlay Program (preschool)

Anyone who spends time with Patty Bourne knows how much she cares about children and young adults. As I pored through this text, it was almost as if she was sitting in the room and having a conversation with me. Patty's practical, down-to-earth approach provides a manual of kid-tested tips and ideas for both the novice and seasoned music educator. It absolutely should be mandatory reading for music majors who plan to teach vocal music. In fact, I'm anxious for it to be published so I can use some of these ideas myself!

—*Dr. Lynn Brinckmeyer*
Director of Choral Music Education
Texas State University

This is a book of 'reality bytes', written by a highly successful teacher of music and children. Patty Bourne writes with honesty and wisdom, with passion and persuasion, and her advice to prospective and newly emerging teachers is rich and worthy of multiple reads until, with attention, the embedded lessons can be fully absorbed. Her points on children, music, lesson plans, singing, and marimba-playing do not just hang there as empty words: they are embedded within stories of real children. She is a master teacher with experience in teaching at various levels and contexts. Thus she knows the field, and she delivers a clear picture of all that it can be in the hands of those who commit themselves to music for children.

—*Dr. Patricia Shehan Campbell*
Donald E. Peterson Professor of Music
University of Washington

Patty Bourne is an inspirational teacher; to her students, their families, colleagues and audiences. Her book now extends that inspiration to a broader music-teaching community, providing concrete advice, practical guidance and an approachable framework for the music classroom.

To watch Patty work with students is to see skill, experience, passion for the art of teaching, love of the learning process, and absolute joy and delight in the opportunity to work with children. Consolidated in her writing you will find the mentoring that we all need, helping to structure our work and teaching so that it can be relevant and motivating.

Be sure to read these words hearing a soft Kentucky accent, the ready smile and easy laughter that is all part of Patty's voice. Here is a teacher with heart, compassion, intelligence, and creativity. What better mentor could there be for all of us working with young people.

—Judith Herrington
Founder and Artistic Director of the Tacoma Youth Chorus
Director of Lower School Music, Charles Wright Academy,
Tacoma, Washington
Composer and Arranger

Patty Bourne's wonderful contribution, *Inside the Music Classroom: Teaching the Art with Heart*, is certain to become one of those very special books that serves as a bold reminder of the cornerstones of the music education profession. While focusing on the "art of the heart" as well as the "heart of the art," the book offers highlights from her own teaching background as well as those of many luminaries who have unselfishly contributed their lives to sharing the joys of music-making. The text is laced with priceless pragmatic suggestions to bring excellence to the rehearsal/classroom setting, and it also is fueled by the spirit-of-*why*. These suggestions are valuable in the ongoing journey of music-learning.

From the first-year teacher to the veteran educator, everyone stands to gain many creative ideas along with a bold shot of inspiration. This is not a book one reads, it is a book one studies; it is certain to become a much-used resource for all those who have dedicated themselves to the availing young minds to the infinite world of music, art, creation. As Patty Bourne asks in the last sentence, "What could be better than that?"

—Dr. Tim Lautzenheiser
President, Attitude Concepts, Inc.
Executive Director of Education,
Conn-Selmer, Inc.

Patty Bourne's *Inside the Music Classroom: Teaching the Art with Heart* is the most practical and inspiring music education book I have read in a long time. Whether you are a pre-service college student, a beginning music teacher, or even a veteran educator in need of re-charging your batteries, this book will become a valued mentor and trail guide.

The book is based on the highly successful music-teaching model established by Patty in her Bothell, WA elementary school and her prior teaching at the university level. When you enter Patty's music classroom, you quickly sense that it is all about kids actively making music in a lively and loving environment. *Inside the Music Classroom* is a storehouse of curriculum ideas, discipline suggestions that work, planning procedures, and helpful hints. You will find right-on-target checklists such as: "Patty's List of Precious P's for Effective Pedagogical Practices," "Tips for Going Inside the Music Class," and "Patty's Pretty Simple Priorities." Don't be deceived by this book's direct and practical tone, it is built on the foundations established by Piaget, Kohlberg, Maslow, Bloom, and others.

I highly recommend this 'must-read' book for anyone starting a career in elementary music education.

—*Will Schmid, Ph.D.*
Past-President, MENC
Professor Emeritus, University of Wisconsin–Milwaukee

Inside the Music Classroom

Teaching the Art with Heart

Patricia Bourne

HERITAGE MUSIC PRESS

A DIVISION OF THE LORENZ CORPORATION
Box 802 / Dayton, OH 45401-0802
www.lorenz.com

Editors: Mary Lynn Lightfoot and Kris Kropff
Book Design: Digital Dynamite, Inc.
Cover Design: Patti Jeffers
Music Engraving: Linda Taylor

Heritage Music Press
A division of The Lorenz Corporation
P.O. Box 802
Dayton, OH 45401-0802
www.lorenz.com

Printed in the United States of America

ISBN: 978-0-89328-560-9

Contents

Preface

I'm one of those educators who thinks about teaching on weekends, on holidays, before and after school. It's not that I don't have a life...I've got a great one! For years, I thought it peculiar (and sort of sad) that I brought my work home, figuratively speaking. I felt guilty about it. If I mentioned the fact that I thought through lessons when hiking, listened to my teenager's music with thoughts of lesson concepts, or wished someone had videotaped a TV segment due to its connection to a skill being taught, many folks would look at me with a 'give it a break, lady' expression on their faces.

Now in my 26th year as an active and full-time music educator, I've finally realized feeling guilty is ridiculous. I've come to accept that I think, read and practice teaching out of genuine passion and excitement for the profession. Teaching is part of who I am as a person. I internalize and exercise the art out of the deep-rooted joy I derive from it.

What's so special about it? When I asked a van full of music educators what they liked best about teaching, their resounding answer was "the kids"—their unlimited abilities, their connectedness with us, and light in their eyes when they understand. The 'best of the best' teachers, who have an unlimited amount of enthusiasm and passion for their profession, think about reaching students: igniting their passions, their motivation to learn and their desire to do better. A superb educator in my school mentioned, "It's kind of a 24-7 deal." What makes it special? The students—*their* learning, *their* energy and *their* potential.

Why this book?

I'm near the end of two and a half decades as a music educator and have taught students preschool through graduate school levels at five locations in four states. Over the course of these years, I've experienced a wide range of occurrences that sparked thoughts and ideas about teaching children more effectively. They've been rattling around in my mind for quite some time, and I'm grateful for the opportunity to write them down in an organized manner.

Why this book? What's it about? Why pick it up in the first place? The intent of this text is to help the reader consider several questions to self:

- What do I think about teaching and the role of the music educator in our schools?
- What might I consider before walking into a room full of students when selecting, developing and implementing curricula or grappling with a discipline or management issue?
- Is there a way to teach the art and rigor of music while balancing that with a heart of one human interacting with another?

This text isn't meant to be a how-to, much less a 'this is it', reference, nor is it filled with witty lessons and activities for students to do. It's more a philosophical narrative of professional perspective from someone who has been active in multiple facets of music education for many years.

Over time, I've come to believe certain things about teachers—their responsibility to and relationship with students and the subsequent learning that occurs in a supportive, heart-and-art-filled classroom environment. Inside the music classroom are students who deserve teachers who think and act with their heads and their hearts. I believe all students have the right to expect music teachers who:

- Want to get to know their students as people and as learners
- Want to show their students ways to think and learn that are healthy, long lasting, and contribute to one's quality of life
- Believe in the academic rigor and artistic uniqueness of music as a subject matter worth discovering
- Realize that they are a part of the fabric in a child's image of what life can be as an adult consumer, contributor and citizen
- Develop a set of strategies, plans and instructional mechanisms where students can be actively engaged, involved and joyful in their growth and understanding

Preparing to Go Inside the Music Classroom

When I taught college methods and subsequently observed graduates enter that first crucial year, I realized that a teacher can only teach what he or she knows how to teach. Most universities do a splendid job of educating the musician: music students graduate from college with proven proficiency as a performer, ensemble member, arranger, theorist, etc. However, they don't, and (in many cases) can't provide an equal balance in pedagogy and instructional methods. Individuals leave the university with the subject matter of music well tooled, while the instructional pieces are marginally diminished.

The good news? Most students who select music education as a major think teaching would be a rewarding career. They've had enough collective experiences in music to envision themselves fitting that role quite nicely. Upon graduating, most music majors have developed a profound commitment to their subject matter and are incredibly eager to share it with students.

What may be lacking is the "Okay, I'm here, ready to go inside, but what do I *really* do now?" part of the job. While it's true that, as Ralph Waldo Emerson wrote, "nothing is ever achieved without enthusiasm," the rookie teacher may have little more than raw enthusiasm to offer. (This was certainly true in my case.) If it's true that a teacher is able to teach only what he or she knows, the subject of music is fairly well learned but the other variables may be lacking: understanding to a significant degree the who, when, how, and why of instructional possibilities.

The 'what do I do now' syndrome comes full bore when the newly hired music educator faces a room of students who are unfamiliar, who enter with mixed anticipation and readiness to be in school, who have varying degrees of attitude and assumptions, and practice habits of mind and body that may or may not be conducive to a friendly interaction. Going into the music classroom can be daunting, disappointing and downright scary when the teacher is uncertain of what to do, how to do it, and to whom to do it.

Going Inside the Book

This book was written in the spirit and hope that it would inform readers of particular issues music educators confront as well as give them thoughts to ponder that might improve instruction. Perhaps by reading this text, or contemplating part of it, some of the edge might be taken off the who, what, when, how, and why of teaching. It's organized into six chapters that take the teacher into the music classroom. Since a majority of my instructional employment has been as an elementary general music specialist (17 years), the scenarios and discussion will reflect that particular setting (K–6, public school).

Chapter 1, "Going Inside the Music Classroom," assumes that an individual has completed some kind of preparation training and is now ready to accept the teacher role. Within this chapter, questions are posed for evaluating one's professional perspective and philosophy as to the role of the music educator in our schools. Suggestions are included that might stimulate thoughts on the multiple facets of teaching music, particularly at the elementary level.

Once inside, there is a hierarchical way of considering the 'what do I do now'. First and foremost, know who's inside. There is a reason why pre-service educators take educational psychology and learn the theories and models of Piaget, Kohlberg, Maslow, Bloom, and Bruner, to name a few. They do begin to make sense as one meets and greets students. Chapter 2, "Who's Inside the Music Classroom?," includes implications and applications of educational theories of thought and research.

When an instructor has a notion of who he or she is teaching, it's time to consider how to organize instruction. Elementary general music teachers have multiple methodologies to employ, as well as diverse (or non-existent) music rooms to serve as teaching environments. Chapter 3, "What's Inside the Music Classroom?," looks at curricula from a content and skills standpoint, rather than advocating a particular methodology. It considers sequence and constructs toward building musicianship.

Chapter 4 is one of the most important chapters in the book. It explores bringing the heart into teaching and keeping it from being hammered away. César Chávez wrote, "A word as to the education of the heart. We don't believe that this can be imparted through books: it can only be imparted through the loving touch of the teacher." It's not easy to remember this when faced with a classroom dynamic that's teetering on disaster! Classroom management is one of the most crucial variables to measure any amount of instructional effectiveness. It can be overwhelming and is often indicated as the greatest single cause for giving up the profession. Music classrooms are particularly unique, when one considers the number of instruments available for touching and the openness of space (rarely have I seen an elementary music classroom with desks and chairs). Developing a management style that fits who one is as a person, but falls within the guidelines of the school and district, is crucial for success and job satisfaction. This chapter is appropriately titled "Bringing Heart Inside the Music Classroom (Without Getting Hammered)."

There is more to a teaching schedule than one class after another, all day long. What about the 'above and beyond' expectations most music teachers fulfill? Programs, special ensembles, a teacher's role as a member of the larger staff, communication with parents, etc. are all part of the gig. Just how do general music teachers put together a PTA event that involves 75 six year olds and live to do it again multiple times? In Chapter 5, "Above and Beyond the Music Classroom," details are shared in regards to developing or maintaining ensembles, as well as timelines and suggestions for producing grade level music programs.

How does a new music educator find the place that fits his personality, teaching style, and encourages professional growth? How does she know it's the right place at the right time? What does it normally take to stay there? What expectations should one have of his administrators? How does *the* place help sustain the energy and stamina required for success? The Chapter 6, "Finding 'It' and Staying in the Music Classroom," looks at a variety of issues pertaining to the job search and satisfaction once employed.

When All Is Said and Done

When all is said and done, this text is intended to remind all music educators, novice and veteran, that teaching in today's music classrooms requires a blend of pedagogical know-how and social savvy. It calls for teachers to find the dignity and rigor in the subject area and break it into practical, purposeful and meaningful instructional steps. It calls for teachers who engage students in memorable experiences that spur further connections and motivation to learn. It calls for a combination of artistic know-how with a heart of caring for the students and their learning. It calls for teachers who remember their priorities that the children in their classrooms are, as Meladee McCarthy wrote, "infinitely more significant than the subject matter we teach."

In his recent book, *The World is Flat: A Brief History of the 21st Century,* Thomas Friedman included sections on the need for igniting both the "curiosity" and "passion" quotients in students. He indicated that together, both exceed and matter more than a student's intelligence quotient, IQ. "...When I think of my favorite teachers, I don't remember the specifics of what they taught me, but I remember being excited about learning it. What has stayed with me are not the facts they imparted but the excitement about learning they inspired."[1]

The focus of the teacher who brings both art and heart into the classroom is on what the students are able to do and the joy they display in doing 'it'. There is always immense satisfaction felt when students show the confidence and enthusiasm that comes from the learning that occurs in the classroom. There's really no better thrill than watching your students engage in music activities with their own passion and energy.

---

[1] Thomas Friedman, *The World is Flat: A Brief History of the 21st Century* (New York: Farrar, Straus, and Giroux, 2006) 303.

They demonstrate the power to "learn how to learn and to love learning."[2]

However, this takes the ability to communicate the art of music with the heart for students. Without heart, there will be no learning. There will be no connection. Because the human brain seeks to repeat that which is pleasing and to avoid, at all costs, that which is miserable. Without the art of music teaching, the music classroom becomes a warm and fuzzy place kids come to, but little more. Do the students know anything? Can they apply music as a subject area? Can they discern quality performances? Can they carry the love and basic knowledge of music into adulthood?

Art and heart must work together so that the students and teacher reap the benefits of all that can occur in each and every music class. Without art, there is no academic substance to stand on, and without heart, it doesn't really mean anything to the educator or learner. While reading this book, I hope you will perceive teaching children as one of the most rewarding, fulfilling professions in humanity and feel better equipped to enter the music classroom with a sense of who you are, what you have to offer students and the intent to develop a classroom filled with joyful learning.

I am grateful for the personal and professional rewards teaching has brought me and for the opportunity to record the 'art and heart' of my experiences in this book. Enjoy your journey into the music classroom.

---

[2] *Ibid.*, 304.

Acknowledgements

This text was completed due to the continuous encouragement of several people. I thank each and every one of these individuals for their efforts and enthusiasm:

- Kris Kropff and the rest of the crew at The Lorenz Corporation
- Mark Mayberry for the wonderful photos and for your consistent support of music education for our mutual students
- Linda Dodge, my neighbor, friend and proofreader extraordinaire
- Angela Kerr, Ted Christensen and Julie Jeppesen for their insight into the world of interviewing and professional development
- Dr. Judi Ford Barber, my first principal, who's passion for people and education fueled my soul for a lifetime
- The student interns and new teachers I've mentored—you *all* provided the impetus and purpose for the creation of this book
- My students and colleagues in Oklahoma, Arizona, Central Washington, and especially those in the Canyon Creek community, Bothell, Washington; thanks for your confidence and support
- Mary Lynn Lightfoot, my dear friend and cheerleader; your enthusiasm for this project was consistently over the top
- To my mother and father, Kathy and Avery Smith, all my love. You were, and still are, the best first teachers a gal could have
- Finally, to my husband, Tom, our daughters Katherine and Julie, and our cat, Tiger; your patience and compassion overflowed at critical times; I am so incredibly proud to be a part of our family. Much love, admiration and appreciation.

Inside the Music Classroom

Going Inside the Music Classroom

The degree is completed and teacher certification requirements met: the new graduate in music education is ready to enter the classroom as teacher, rather than student/observer/ student intern. What a major step! Going inside the classroom as the 'main' teacher is an exceedingly different experience than going in as observer or intern.

One is now expected to be able to:

1. Organize instruction
2. Manage a classroom
3. Communicate with all constituents (students, parents, district and building colleagues)

Furthermore, he or she should:

4. Understand the social and political realities of the profession
5. Comprehend content and skills to teach in an age-appropriate manner (quite a task at the elementary level, with the span of preschool to puberty entering the room)
6. Establish and maintain an environment that is conducive to learning
7. Develop a plan for continuing education and professional growth

No longer the student-in-training, the new graduate is now the *teacher*; in truth, however, the graduate's learning has just begun. A degree in hand qualifies the person, but the

3

person is responsible for bringing quality to the profession. How does it start?

"Who Are You?"

As one enters the music class, knowing who he or she is as a person is vital. While complete self-knowledge is a life-long pursuit, understanding some basics about oneself—strengths, shortcomings, passions and beliefs—provides a foundation for success as a teacher.

Personality most definitely plays a role in being effective as an instructor. After all, one's personality is the filter naturally employed when faced with choices and alternative actions. As a teacher within the music classroom, an educator will make multiple decisions, often within a split second. He or she may not have the luxury of time to consider all possible courses of action through any other lens but his or her own.

The ultimate goal, I believe, is for teachers to be honest and authentic, to be true to who they are as people. Good teachers indicate that when they try to be someone they're not, the students see right through it; furthermore, they can't maintain the energy it takes to imitate and act out a role. Teaching is an extension of who a person is in the 'real' world. Good teachers know how to be themselves and bring the best of themselves into the learning arena. Every successful classroom in the country became successful due to the adult personality in the room; nothing else compares.

Once the music classroom is entered, it's all about the teacher and the students. Learning occurs as a result of the relationship the effective educator develops with students, as well as how he or she organizes what it is they will do. When I remember my best teachers, I'm certain they became favorites due to what they taught, how they taught, and the relationship we developed within the educational setting. These teachers were comfortable showing us who they were as people. I believe the combination of personality plus professional know-how is the essence of a good and memorable teacher.

Richard Traina, president of Clark University, shared three characteristics that describe a good teacher:

1. Competence in subject matter
2. Caring deeply about students and their success
3. Distinctive character[1]

[1] James H. Stronge, *Qualities of Effective Teachers* (Alexandria, VA: Association of Supervision and Curriculum Development, 2002).

This "distinctive character" is the unique personality one brings into the classroom. Stronge indicated that as a person, an effective teacher makes a habit of:

1. Listening to, understanding, and knowing students
2. Establishing a fair and respectful environment
3. Promoting enthusiasm and motivation for learning[2]

I've observed that most successful music teachers are generally quite passionate about their subject matter. How can one teach something from the depth of his soul unless genuinely enthused about it? (I've experienced teachers who didn't care much for their own subject matter; it's not easy to learn in that kind of setting.) The magic of teaching occurs when we see a transformation in our students as they progress in their genuine love for learning and for music. This can only occur when a teacher's distinctive character is blended with a rich learning environment.

Questions to Self

I think teachers should take the time to ask themselves certain questions to trigger self-awareness and professional perspective. The answers should help guide educational decisions teachers encounter throughout their career. Before going inside the music classroom, consider asking:

1. What do I believe about learners?
2. What is my fundamental reason for teaching music in a school/classroom setting?
3. What do I have to offer as a teacher and as a colleague?
4. What personal qualities and traits do I possess that will help me succeed? That will help my students succeed?
5. What do I believe a successful teacher looks like and sounds like?
6. What does joyful learning look like and sound like?
7. How do I want my students to describe me as a teacher and as a person?
8. What honor do I bring to the profession?
9. Am I ready to put my own musician ego aside and allow my students to be the 'stars'?

---

[2] *Ibid.*

10. Do I have the confidence in myself to seek the assistance and support I will undoubtedly need from others?

I'm sure many of these questions have been raised and discussed in graduate classes and music teacher workshops. They are worth revisiting, regardless of accumulated years as an educator. They are particularly worth asking when redirection or renewal is needed. Students deserve the best we have to offer; now and then, we all need reminders of why we chose this particular career.

The First of Many Firsts

When one elects to be a music educator, he or she must understand that a teacher will be part of a child's history and reality. A teacher is part of the fabric that forms a young person's opinion of what adults do and how they function in the world. It's a powerful responsibility that can either bless or haunt both teacher and child.

I recall with a slight bit of embarrassment how poorly I communicated information in my first years as an elementary general music teacher. I'm especially embarrassed when I think of how I dressed and how I reacted to things. (I wish I'd asked myself the above questions repeatedly 25 years ago.) But I was fortunate to have begun my teaching career with an incredible principal who encouraged me by saying, "The kids know you care about your subject and that you care about them and their learning. The rest will come." She helped me realize that at a novice level, I was fulfilling a crucial role for the students: at a minimum level, I *was* the adult in the room and I *did* want to be their teacher. As my first administrator/mentor, she consistently boosted my confidence with reminders that keeping one's heart, eyes and mind on the learners is the most important skill to possess.

In the Beginning

Deep down, I always believed I was on the right career path, but those first few years were often just plain scary. I wasn't exactly sure what to do, when to do it, how to do it, or why do it at all. Instinct and enthusiasm carried me only so far. When I remember my first year of teaching, the memories are either overly illuminated or dreadfully dark. While it was thrilling to actually be a certified, employed music educator, I felt terribly insecure and lacked confidence. I recall thinking "Oh yeah!" and "Oh help!" within the same breath.

Going inside the room a month before students arrived was easy and exciting. It was clean from a summer's attention and bright with high expectations. The bulletin boards were begging for my creative juices to flow. I entered the room with a great deal of confidence. I played the instruments, looked through and began filling my teacher's desk, and made sure there was plenty of chalk and that the erasers were reasonably clean. The Basel series texts were lined up on the shelves, color-coded so that I could tell one grade from the other. I wanted to be ready, and wasn't quite sure if I was.

I had a schedule, a roster for each class, and a magnificently written lesson plan. The district supplied plenty of materials and resources for my use. My principal and colleagues were encouraging and supportive of me. Everything was in place for success.

But, here I was, inside the music class with students coming. This was no longer a 'practice' run-through. This was no longer just a music class I'd prepared for, but a *music class with real children*! The butterflies in my stomach exceeded those I'd experienced on stage in junior and senior recitals.

My first lesson for them quickly became a dynamic and memorable lesson for *me*. I'd arranged carpet squares in a circle and had placed the appropriate grade-level textbook on each carpet square. In walked the students. The first student to enter my first classroom was a fourth grader named Andrea. She sized me up, looked at the books neatly arranged on the neatly organized carpet squares and curled her lip. The first words uttered to me from a student were, "We don't like those books, and those carpet squares stink." The entire line smugly agreed with their line leader.

Thus began my indoctrination into the life of a music teacher. It could have been worse. It could have been better, but it was a start. When I stopped being nervous each and every day, I felt increasingly more comfortable applying more and more of 'me' into my instruction. It became easier to set routines that provided starting points for the students: no more dirty carpet squares.

I was also extremely fortunate to be surrounded by a group of master teachers who did not hesitate to answer my requests for advice. I believe the support (and patience) I received from colleagues, mentors and a fantastic building principal not only made the first years successful, but probably helped confirm that this profession was the right choice for me.

I appreciate with profound gratitude the many ways I was helped and encouraged during my novice period. They guided me to structure, in my mind and heart, the image of the teacher I wanted to be without sacrificing who I was as a person and without forcing me to duplicate someone else's 'program'. They helped me develop professional and personal perspective that I've relied on throughout my career.

Building a Professional Profile

In social gatherings, I always find it interesting to describe what I do for a living to other people, especially non-educators. A typical conversation would be as follows:

Person: "So, what do you do?"
Me: "I'm a teacher."
Person: "Oh, what do you teach?"
Me: "Music."
Person: "That must be fun."

The conversation then proceeds to what the other person does.

What I would *like* to say is, "I teach children. My subject area is music, but I design lessons and instructional materials to help my students learn to think, to apply and to create so that they might expand the quality of their lives and the lives of others."

Obviously, not everyone has the time for that kind of answer. But, that's what I believe fully describes what I do and why I do it. I'd like to be able to articulate, in every career dialogue, how deeply committed I am to students and how privileged I am to be a part of this extended period of their young lives.

The 15 "P's"

As this philosophical description of what I do and why I do it has evolved (over 26 years), so has a professional list I refer to as *Patty's List of Precious P's for Effective Pedagogical Practices*. These "P" words have helped guide and mold my conversations with myself as I've entered a variety of music classes. I presented a session on four of these "P's" at a conference quite a few years ago and was delighted to read an entire chapter of 30 "P's" in Peter Boonshaft's book, *Teaching Music with Passion: Conducting, Rehearsing and Inspiring.* I definitely encourage the reader to devour Dr. Boonshaft's entire book, as I have. It's a magnificent resource. Giving a nod to him, as well as Webster's dictionary, here are my 15 "P's."

1. Personality: The distinctive qualities and traits of an individual

One's personality can't help but influence who he will be as a teacher. It's difficult to fake it—students have an amazing ability to recognize faking at any level. Does it mean that one must sometimes play the role of the teacher? Absolutely, especially when fatigue or frustration set in. All teachers experience those episodes now and then; however, when one's true personality is confident, convincing, and "distinctive," children will respond and appreciate the real person behind the teacher face.

2. Perspective: An idea of the relative importance of things

During the first years of teaching, developing perspective is particularly tough. Everything is magnified, and it's not easy to determine which challenge requires attention *right now*. There are so many decisions to make as a teacher; one must develop perspective so that she can keep her head above the water, so to speak. Daily issues that require thought and action confront every teacher. Not every problem is easy to solve, but with perspective, one can more easily sort things out.

3. Patience: The habit of being patient, tolerant, steadfast, understanding

Learning takes time. Each student has his own personal filter that determines what will be learned when. Waiting and watching for students to show the light bulb of understanding can be wearying. When I was in my first years of teaching, I made extra money cutting grass—the immediate gratification of a job well done was such a relief as compared to the delayed gratifications of teaching. Teaching takes patience. Learning takes patience. Remain steadfast and resolute, and measure success in small increments.

4. Predisposition: A tendency to behave in a particular way

Something magical begins to develop after a few successful months of teaching. The effective educator begins to predict what could, or probably will, occur in any given activity and can be predisposed to design instruction that brings about positive results. Students are also predisposed to act and/or react in certain ways. The more the teacher knows her students and their predispositions, the more she's able to manage and direct instruction.[3]

5. Prioritize: To regard or handle things according to their importance

Effective educators establish priorities for instruction and classroom dynamic throughout their career. I maintain three basic priorities, or goals, for what I want students to learn (see Chapter 3) and only two basic priorities for the classroom environment (see Chapter 4). Priorities offer direction and focus for an overall educational plan. A lack of priorities can turn instruction into the 'willy-nilly/come what may' classroom, which won't necessarily lead to deep learning or meaning.

6. Preparation: The state of readiness for some purpose or task

How ready is the teacher to walk into the music classroom? What opportunities were offered and taken advantage of in order to be as prepared as one can be for the teaching profession? One of my greatest 'should-a, would-a, could-a' regrets is that I didn't spend enough time in classrooms observing kids before I took my first job. I was not ready pedagogically (or psychologically) for what I was asked to do.

Another preparatory step I wish I'd pursued was to have conversations with new teachers. I did not take advantage of these opportunities and know now what a difference they would have made. New teachers describe their early experiences in terms that cannot replicated by one with veteran status; they offer perspective on what teaching is really like.

---

[3] See Chapters 2 and 4 for more on this topic.

7. Passion: The object of intense interest and/or enthusiasm

What happens in an effective classroom? An adult's passion for subject matter and student learning, paralleled with the heart of the educational process, is obvious for all to see and feel. Passion grows from who the teacher is and what he or she believes. It's probably the most honest reflection of one's personality. The teacher who generates excitement motivates students to get excited too. In most cases, the students respond to the passionate teacher with energy and a sense of adventure. What happens in classrooms where passion for subject and learning is evident? Joy!

8. Preference: The opportunity for choosing one course of action over the other

Teachers have a right to share their preferences, especially in music. As a new teacher, my musical preferences spanned multiple styles. I had a large record collection that I was anxious to share with students. In addition, my mother was a physical education teacher who emphasized movement and dance; therefore, moving to music, with organized steps or free motion, was something I comfortably embraced.

I believe we instruct best through our own comfort zones, particularly when teaching is so new. Blending one's preferences with materials and resources available makes sense. Effective teachers also consider their students' preferences and will often find creative ways to incorporate those into lessons.

9. Practice: To do something repeatedly in order to improve performance

Musicians know all about practicing! What we forget is the amount of time we need to practice teaching: practice indeed leads to smoother transitions, tighter lesson structure, and clearer communication.

Practicing is also a disposition educators focus on with students. Regardless of their age, repeated practice, doled out in age-appropriate time frames, is irreplaceable. Most teachers of very young children tire of repeating things long before the students, but they realize their students' brains require that repetition to begin to connect and move forward.

Practice the craft of teaching and help students practice so that they may learn and remember.

10. Prediction: Forming an opinion about what will happen in the future

This "P" can prevent lessons from imploding. Once a teacher gets to know the students and has established his classroom setting, the power of prediction helps foresee possible management issues. Prediction allows one to sense whether a specific lesson is going to sail or sink.

Maria Callas wrote, "The difference between good teachers and great teachers is this: good teachers make the best of a pupil's means. Great teachers foresee a pupil's ends." This particular "P" may take a while to become well seasoned, but it becomes a powerful ally.

11. Positive Outlook: The disposition to expect the best possible outcome

I really do believe that optimists tend to become teachers, or perhaps, effective teachers practice optimism. How can any reasonable educator face a class of students hour after hour and think, "I know this will fail. The kids won't get it; they'll all think I'm stupid. They'll probably start talking anyway, so I might as well not even try."?

What one expects to occur will normally occur. What one expects students to do, or to say, will usually come true as well. Optimists find the students ready to learn and consider each day filled with potential.

12. Participation: The act of taking part in a given activity, or sharing in something

Participating in school activities is something effective teachers do. Whether it's their willingness to help out at the school barbeque, sponsor the chess club, or serve on the search and rescue squad, participation as a member of the whole staff is imperative. Likewise, students need to learn and understand what participation looks like (see Chapter 4). If they know what's expected from them as a participant, their actions are clearer and have a defined purpose. Ultimately, learning music requires participation—one cannot learn it without a level of personal investment.

13. Perseverance: To continue in an action or belief, despite difficulties or setbacks

During my first year of teaching, I would walk to a specific restaurant on Saturdays for their buffet breakfast. I would eat and read the paper and look at the various people in the room. I used to think, "These folks are so lucky: they don't have to worry about what they'll do on Monday. They just go to their jobs, do their 'thing' for 8 hours, and go home, free and clear of troubles." Sometimes, I coveted the job of a convenience store worker! But colleagues kept saying, "Hang in there! We're with you! You'll make it!" They taught me the meaning of perseverance, particularly when the roadblocks were my own limitations. Find a way to make it work, rely on supporters, persevere, and don't quit.

14. Playfulness: The state of having fun, high spirits, lively

Peggy Bennett wrote that playfulness "implies an openness to possibility."[4] She further indicates that a playful attitude allows for "moments of fun and unexpected outcomes."[5] It allows for the children to see their teachers as members of the community, perhaps not always the one in control. "Through playfulness, imaginations are cultivated."[6]

Some of my favorite memories of specific lessons are linked to the playful atmosphere hanging in the air. Laughter and liveliness lighten the intensity and mood of the classroom. It really is okay to be silly when silliness is a human reaction or trigger for whatever is occurring. (The first time I really belly-laughed in a kindergarten classroom, I rolled backwards with delight; the students piled on top of me! Literally!) Being playful is a sign of a healthy human being; Maturity outlines and frames how that playfulness can be displayed.

15. Professionalism: The competence, or character expected of highly trained professionals

To be called into the profession of teaching is often promoted. However, to be called into and walked all over isn't very professional. If we believe what we do is noble and deserves the respect it's due, then we need to behave in ways that

---

[4] Peggy Bennett, "The Heart of Singing" (paper presented at the Symposium on Singing, New York, 2006), 1.

[5] *Ibid.*, 2.

[6] *Ibid.*

offer the image of a professional. We need to expect to treat others as one professional treats another. Walk the walk, talk the talk, dress the part, and be an advocate for this profession. "Only teachers can take the dignity out of teaching and only teachers can put it back. It depends, therefore, on the manner in which teachers conduct themselves."[7]

Above-and-beyond promotion of our profession will do more for the craft than anything else. Go to professional meetings. Belong to professional groups (and there are many). Subscribe to professional texts and journals. Dignify the profession through action and involvement.

This list of "P's" serves merely as guideposts for the reader to consider when pondering the music education 'business.' Obviously, the job itself is profoundly complex with multiple variables. The more you know and think about it before entering, the more effective you will be.

Tips for Going Inside the Music Class

Entering the music classroom combines the best efforts of one's preparation with the personal attributes he or she brings to teaching. While the first year can be overwhelming, the new teacher learns to rely on strengths of self and others.

I think my first years would have been more successful had I considered the elementary experience more thoughtfully as an undergraduate. Simple things would have helped. I offer these simple tips for consideration in preparation for entering the music class:

Tip #1. Watch them grow

Teaching music at the elementary level requires an understanding of the preschool to pubescent brain. As a school's music teacher, one has the opportunity to be a part of a child's development from a very young age to a time when he or she stands eye-to-eye with you, height-wise. If a teacher remains in a single location long enough, he or she has a history with each child that is long lasting and unique. The music teacher in an elementary school is fortunate to witness a student's growth in profound and insightful ways. What a privilege!

---

[7] Eph Ehly, *Hogey's Journey* (Dayton, OH: Heritage Music Press, 2006), 36.

Tip #2. Teach healthy habits

One has an opportunity to teach healthy habits of brain, body and soul. From year to year, music educators teach breath support, healthy posture, a predisposition to look for and recognize beauty, a celebration of creativity, and an appreciation of artistic wonder. Children begin to describe and do what is necessary to generate *music*, not just sound. Once established as habits, children practice and process procedures that they'll remember year to year: They tell themselves, "In this music room, I…" "When I want to sing well, I can…" "In order to get a great sound from this instrument, I should…" "When I do this, I can expect to…"

The good news? Habits of body, mind and soul are established for a lifetime. The bad news? Habits of body, mind and soul are established for a lifetime; just ask anyone who was asked at any point in their life to simply mouth the words. Be purposeful and consistent in the habits selected to reinforce, and always remember the person inside.

Tip #3. Be ready to do it all

Elementary music teachers do it all. They teach everyone, regardless of placement, grade, skill, or cognitive abilities. They teach all facets of music skills—singing, listening, playing, composing, improvising, reading and writing music, following conducting gestures, and moving to and responding to music. They quickly discover how to generate enthusiasm from their students in developmentally appropriate ways. They communicate with classroom teachers on a routine basis. They see students year after year and look for signs that they've taught them something.

Doing it all is a dizzying aspect to the job of the elementary music teacher. It also calls for a strong musician with varying degrees of proficiency in multiple skills in music. Strengthening one's musical abilities in a variety of ways will be time well spent. During my first job interview, an assistant superintendent in Oklahoma leaned back in his chair, propped his size-14 boots on his desk, and grilled me about my limited piano skills. As a new teacher, his concern about my limited playing ability prompted me to spend the first three years of teaching elementary music taking lessons to improve. It was definitely worth the effort as it resulted in an expanded repertoire of what I was able to offer my students (as well as helping me become a stronger musician).

Tip #4. Keep track of the schedule

The daily schedule of the elementary music teacher is constant. For the most part, one meets back-to-back classes—one class exits while the other enters. Sometimes, it isn't easy to shake off the previous lesson while simultaneously preparing for the next.

In order to help organize my day, I write an outline of each lesson on the whiteboard so that I'm clear on who's coming and what they might need. When the class finishes and a short break occurs, I try to jot a few notes in my plan book that will guide any revisions or repetitions needed when a particular class returns later in the week. Sometimes I must wait a couple of hours to complete this task, but the payoff is worth it.

My advice? Talk with other general music teachers about their daily schedule. Assume that there are multiple ways to affect who comes when. If the school has a scheduling committee, by all means be a member of it, or chair it, if possible. If the building administrator designs the schedule, then suggest alternatives that could result in improvements, if appropriate to do so. The goal is to give students the best opportunities to learn. What needs to occur in the schedule to offer the children the most optimal experiences?

Tip #5. Be proactive with overall health and stamina

The elementary general music teacher uses his or her voice all day long and must learn the art of pacing. By the end of the day, have something left for the kids who are eager to enter the class. For me, elementary music teaching tends to be a very physical profession. I'm on my feet, dancing, singing, moving instruments, distributing materials, talking, leading, and encouraging. Reserving the energy needed for that last class requires self-monitoring throughout the day.

It's vital to maintain one's health (although very difficult to do, particularly that first year). Immunities will build over time. The new teacher should take the time to get in shape, vocally and physically. Drink water to keep the vocal cords strong. Sleep!

I've learned that teaching when I am vocally or physically tired is not very satisfying to the students, nor to me. The physical journey from being a passive undergraduate student in a class to being the teacher in charge is profound. Learn to breathe.

Tip #6. No one's perfect

Final tip for going inside the music classroom: Accept the fact that mistakes will be made. All educators meet with failure in some areas of the job. Every fantastic teacher I've talked with has had moments of disaster. Don't let them become stumbling blocks to the long-range vision of what can be offered. Mentors, colleagues and administrators want to see new teachers succeed and are eager to offer assistance. Ask for advice.

Going inside the music classroom with a degree only provides the license to be there. But entering with a sense of who one is and what is believed about teaching extends beyond the degree and certification. We all have the opportunity to bring the best part of us as people into the teaching arena. Place time and emphasis on discovering self, then, imagine that 'self' as an effective teacher of children.

When the butterflies of the first year erupt, be secure in knowing thousands of teachers experience the same feeling. After 26 years, I still get butterflies (more from excitement than nervousness, though). Connect with the kids, be real, apply strengths, seek advice, and enjoy this journey.

Who's Inside the Music Classroom?

Good teaching starts with knowing one's own personality as well as the strengths and qualities you bring to the classroom. It's equally crucial that the instructor learns as much as possible about *who* his or her students are as learners and as people. All educators should begin with a basic sense of the developmental, emotional and psychological frameworks that operate in their students. What we know about our learners *before* starting the job prompts more successful interactions between teacher and child.

Just as a good market analyst studies the target group most likely to purchase a particular product, or a coach maintains countless statistics that might affect the outcome of a game, successful and effective teachers strive to know and understand their population. Doing so initiates perspective and insight into how one's students will react, progress, behave, and succeed.

Knowing who is taught goes beyond understanding the chronological, sociological and developmental ages of one's students. It includes knowing the community, the culture and previous music experiences, as well as the cognitive and physical abilities or limitations of the children. The teachers who consistently meet their students 'where they are' as well as 'who they are' tend to experience success.

Effective educators ask questions of fellow staff members, survey the neighborhood—Where do the students live? Where do their parents shop?—and look through remaining information that offers a glimpse of a previous music teachers' emphasis. They seek to implement what they know about children, via study or experience, with what they see in the surrounding area of their school.

19

Sometimes, the population and/or community will shift. School districts may alter boundary lines, elect different models for best serving special-needs students, or change transportation routes. Over the summer, things can change within a school. (This experience occurred in my case; read further in this chapter for details.) Effective educators continually update information about their students and understand that there could be changes affecting who will actually walk through their door in September.

Over the course of time, teachers may see differences in their population that indicate social shifts. In 26 years of teaching, I've certainly witnessed changes in the childhood experience. Students of the 21st century are mixed with diversity well beyond what the eyes can perceive. Fundamental knowledge of how *all* students learn (based on what we currently know about the brain and what is available for adapting instruction for special needs children) is not only valuable to know, but leads to better instruction.

This chapter includes an overview of who's in the music classroom through a variety of lenses. It is intended to provide a broad scope of theoretical and practical ways to understand the students we teach. What makes our students tick? What learning characteristics are developmentally programmed? How can teachers become more aware of their students' level of comprehension? How can music educators structure classes to fulfill the diversity of students entering their room?

Educational Psychology: Relevance and Reality for the Music Educator

How do we begin the process of knowing whom we're teaching before learning the specifics (neighborhood environment, suburb vs. urban vs. rural, etc.)? Within teacher-education curricula, the theories and models of educational psychologists are included for this very purpose. Future educators are introduced to the writings and research of individuals who contributed to the understanding of the developing minds, bodies and souls of children. Names like Piaget, Kohlberg, Maslow, and Bloom; Bruner, Watson, Skinner, and Erikson; Locke, Dewey, Pavlov, and Freud are mentioned in pre-service training so that educators have an opportunity to understand the learner in general terms, prior to entering the classroom.

There are many influential writers, scientists, psychologists, and educators who have written on various aspects of education and each has provided theories of considerable importance and value for music educators. Within this chapter, I'll include theories and empirical examples of Piaget, Kohlberg, Maslow, and Bloom. In Chapter 3, Bruner is referred to for his influential theories of instruction. These five educator/researcher/psychologists represent a wide spectrum of thoughts and constructs regarding child development, motivation for learning, and cognitive skill acquisition.

Perhaps one of the reasons teacher-preparation programs include educational psychology classes is so new graduates have references to fall back on when faced with instructional dilemmas affected by who they are teaching. It wasn't always clear to me, as an undergraduate, why I was studying theories of development and learning. The connection between what 'ed psych' had to offer and what might help me understand my students wasn't clear in my mind.

Ten years after graduating, I was the one teaching college music methods and still didn't get the real connection between educational theory and classroom settings. I didn't choose to include theories of development in my instruction of college music majors. After all, that was taken care of in the education and psychology buildings!

One particular day, I observed a music education student instruct a mini-lesson to a class of pre-school students. I finally got it! Something occurred in that lesson that helped me begin to associate instructional methods with the relevancy of the theories and models of educational psychology.

The lesson I observed involved an undergraduate 21-year-old male student and 4-year-old children. This particular college student was a very fine musician with superb jazz saxophone 'chops'. Following my lead and request for methods students to bring themselves and their passions to their instruction, he chose to use his saxophones for a lesson on high and low.

He began by playing a short riff on the baritone sax (the largest of the four) and repeated the same riff on the tenor, the alto, and the soprano (the smallest). After all four instruments were played, he set them on their floor stands and asked, "Okay kids! Which is highest?" The four year olds confidently pointed to the baritone sax. "That one!," they agreed in unison.

Slightly bewildered, this budding music educator repeated the process, exaggerating the lowest tones on the baritone sax, as well as emphasizing the high sounds of the soprano. Once again, the question was asked. "Which instrument is the highest and which is the lowest?" And again, the children answered as they had before, pointing to the baritone as the highest and the soprano as the lowest.

In their minds, and with their level of understanding, they were right. After all, the biggest/tallest, and, therefore, the highest off the ground (while on the floor stand) was the baritone. Their expressions were priceless: "Why doesn't this guy get it? It's very clear to us which is highest and lowest."

Good lesson for this fellow and a wonderful chance for his classmates to observe the pre-operational mind of the four-and-a-half year old. Piaget would have loved this demonstration.

Piaget and his Cognitive Development Theory

Jean Piaget studied and observed children while working at the Beset Laboratory in Paris (circa 1920). According to Crain, Piaget's job was to administer intelligence tests to young children.[1] During the process of questioning the kids, he became interested in the actual responses being given, particularly the 'wrong ones' offered up by the youngest participants.

Intrigued by the workings of the young mind, Piaget was one of the first scientists to publicly speculate that young chil-

---

[1] William Crain, *Theories of Development: Concepts and Applications* (Englewood Cliffs, NJ: Prentice-Hall, Inc., 1985).

dren aren't 'dumber' than older children (or adults for that matter), but that they think in extremely different ways.[2] Back in the '20s and '30s, this was a revolutionary idea. After all, children were expected to be seen and not heard during this era.

Over the course of his studies and observations, Piaget identified four stages children pass through. Since this book is primarily intended for music teachers in a K–6 setting, I'll focus on stages II (*pre-operational*), III (*concrete operations*) and IV (*formal operations*). These particular stages are observable and applicable to the ages taught in K–6.

Piaget's Theory Within the Music Class

One of Piaget's discoveries was that young children equate life with any kind of object (which explains why, at the age of three or four, I thought my food had feelings and would take the remainder of my breakfast to my dresser so that it wouldn't feel 'left out'. I was particularly worried about my leftover pancakes…).

---

[2] Renate Caine, and Geoffrey Caine, *Making Connections: Teaching and the Human Brain* (Menlo Park, CA: Addison-Wesley Publishing Company, 1994) 89.

This notion of life in all objects is especially apparent in my kindergarten and first-grade students. The children are quite eager to know the name of all the instruments in the room— not just that it's a drum or it's a guitar, rather its *personal* name. They have helped name several of the instruments. My guitar, Wilma, is greeted with a "Hello, Wilma" every time I play it. The kids inevitably ask if my other guitar, Fred, is feeling well since he's not the one selected to play. This ritual occurs day-in, day-out. Likewise, when the children play one of the barred instruments in the room, they want to know whether it's Shiny, Sandy, Tall Guy, Big Daddy, or Newbie.

Our second graders love calling the instruments by name, but they no longer give the instruments lifelike qualities. They gleefully play away without the same reference and expressions of greeting and affinity so often seen with the younger students.

By the age of eight or so, children begin to understand that life exists in those things that move on their own, namely plants and animals. From third grade on, the care of the instruments is taken into consideration, but passing on lifelike feelings has passed; it's no longer part of their cognitive being. By this time, the students want to apply the real name to the instrument (the djembe, the metallophone, the guiro). The personal names disappear as the children travel from the pre-operations stage to the concrete stage.

By the formal operations stage (roughly age 10 or 11 and older), students' thinking soars. They enter the realm of abstract and theoretical thought. They can look at and apply considerable possibilities to tasks. When students reach this stage, they are ready for units involving self-directed (independent or group) projects.

At the formal operations stage, the possibilities of applying concepts and skills are limitless, particularly if presented in an organized and choice-filled manner. Students are capable of revising, rethinking and reviewing; they can consider if-then scenarios. They are usually excited to use their brainpower, especially when the foundations have been laid for success.

There are profound differences in the pre-operational vs. formal operations child, especially in regard to ego and egocentric thinking. Recently, I asked a first-grade class why they thought I'd taught them a song game (one they all enjoyed learning and participating in). The responses included, "'Cause we've been good!" "'Cause it was a fun thing to do!"

"'Cause we got to run and you like to see us happy!" It took several prompts and direct examples for them to realize it was a *song* game—it included singing, moving and listening—I, as the music teacher, had included for learning purposes.

Describing the why of something couldn't be referenced to anyone but themselves: Their egocentric brains couldn't look at it from another perspective. In contrast, 45 minutes later, I asked a group of sixth graders to describe the ways learning to play the guitar is such a powerful social and personal endeavor. The answers showed in-depth understanding and worldliness. "When you play the guitar, you can make all the music yourself." "Sometimes playing chords while someone else plays the melody makes the music that much better." "I think we're learning to play the guitar so that we can understand all parts of music better; it gives us a way to apply what we're learning."

Effective teachers ask questions of their students to gain perspective of what their students know as well as to learn who they are. The answers to these questions are couched in what the children are capable of knowing within their developmental level.

The human mind is a marvel! Elementary music teachers are fortunate to witness, firsthand, the transition from one Piagetian stage to the next.

Kohlberg's Stages of Moral Development

While his name may not be as recognizable as Piaget, Lawrence Kohlberg's findings certainly impact how teachers understand whom they are teaching. Kohlberg was born in New York in 1927 and, as a young man, displayed academic brilliance, earning his bachelor's degree in one year. As a graduate student in psychology, he became interested in Piaget's stage theory, particularly in terms of how children perceive and reference issues of trust, judgment, dilemma, and right vs. wrong.

Kohlberg uncovered phases of moral development while interviewing samples of children (conducted first in 1958 and continuing in 1963 and 1970). The basic interview consisted of a series of dilemmas told in stories. An example included one called "Heinz Steals the Drug."

In Europe, a woman was near death from a special kind of cancer. There was one drug that the doctors thought might save her. It was a form of radium that a druggist in the same town had recently discovered. The drug was expensive to make, but the druggist was charging ten times what the drug cost him to make. He paid $200 for the radium and charged $2,000 for a small dose of the drug. The sick woman's husband, Heinz, went to everyone he knew to borrow the money, but he could get together (only) about $1,000 which is half of what it cost. He told the druggist that his wife was dying and asked him to sell it cheaper or let him pay later. But the druggist said: "No, I discovered the drug and I'm going to make money from it." So Heinz got desperate and broke into the man's store to steal the drug for his wife. Should the husband have done that?[3]

A yes or no answer was not what Kohlberg was after; rather, he was looking for the *reasoning* behind the answer. How would children rationalize and sort through what was right and was wrong based on this story? Tested over time (1950s through 1970s), Kohlberg identified six stages. The first four generally encompass children who are in the elementary levels:

Stage 1: Obedience and Punishment Orientation

Authorities hand down a set of rules that must be followed. Punishment is a result and something to be avoided at all costs.

Stage 2: Individualism and Exchange

Different individuals have different viewpoints and should be free to pursue individual interests. Punishment is simply a risk one wants to avoid.

Stage 3: Conventional Morality

Good behavior is linked to good motives—concern for others, doing what the family or relationship would generally see as right—despite possible punishment.

Stage 4: Maintain the Social Order

Emphasis is on obeying laws and respecting authority for the good of society as a whole. Conception of the function of laws for greater purpose (than to avoid punishment, as in Stage 1).

---

[3] Crain, 120.

Kohlberg's Theory and Its Impact on Who's in the Music Class

Crain summarizes that at Stage 1, children think of right and wrong as what authority says. Avoiding punishment is the goal. At Stage 2, children now see that there are different sides to any issue: Making deals and exchanging favors is a useful way to avoid direct punishment. Finally, at Stages 3 and 4, young people begin to reason as members of the whole society; being a good person and motivated to obey laws to maintain the social climate is vital.

How does Kohlberg's theory impact who we are teaching in the music class? In Chapter 4, "Bringing Heart Inside the Music Classroom (Without Getting Hammered)," stories are told that have a direct impact on management, consequences and rules of order. The reader will undoubtedly draw parallels between Kohlberg's stages and the action of the children referred to in those stories. Moral issues are naturally linked to management systems. I've witnessed a number of occurrences in music classes that directly relate to the manner used to solve dilemmas at particular stages:

- Walking into the music room, first grader, Peter, walks directly to a drum and plays it, rather than go directly to his circle spot as instructed. Classmate Charlie reports, "Mrs. Bourne! Peter just played the drum." (A bit of information I, obviously, already knew.) "Peter, what were the instructions?" Peter replies, showing that he knows what he was supposed to do, but admits he "made a mistake." The punishment? Go back and enter again, without the drum playing. It wasn't a major issue—it was simply a mistake, as he admitted. Problem solved.
- Two third graders are working on rhythm dictation, sharing small manipulatives with rhythmic notation on each. I've instructed the class to decide whether they'll work together on the task or take turns, as I have a limited number of the manipulatives. Jane and Josh agree to take turns. When Jane lays out her rhythms incorrectly, Josh charges in to correct her. Jane reports, "Hey Mrs. Bourne! Josh and I decided we'd take turns, but now he wants to do all of it!" "Well, I'm just trying to help. She can help me, too, if she wants." You scratch my back—I'll scratch yours. Rath-

er than be split up, the dilemma was met with negotia-
tion. Problem solved.

• In a sixth-grade classroom, Jaime designates herself as
the leader of her group of three students. They are
working on a composition that has specific criteria to
be included, and Jaime is anxious to get it right. Allison
and Archie don't necessarily appreciate, or agree, that
Jaime should make all the decisions. It's a dilemma,
but one that can be handled through discussion and
revisiting the task at hand. Issues need to be resolved
so that the trio can accomplish the task in a way such
that the whole group will be equally satisfied with both
process and product. With very little redirection from
me, the group handles the problem with Jaime by reviewing the purpose of the project. They agreed they
must have input to create a product that included the
criteria but was reflective of all three members. They
end up with a great composition. Problem solved.

Kohlberg's stages are not directly linked to, or natural products of, maturation; they are, however, the result of interaction and mental processes. As children socialize and learn with others, they learn how viewpoints differ, they learn to discuss their problems, and they discover multiple ways to work out any differences that exist. "The less children feel pressured simply to conform to authority, the freer they are to settle their own differences and formulate their own ideas."[4]

By understanding how children respond to moral issues of right vs. wrong, the stronger our skills become at structuring the learning environment so that children can learn to grapple with moral issues in a motion that inspires forward thinking. Kohlberg's theories allow educators to bear witness to the multiple and complex phases of this development, rather than identifying character traits that may be not quite true ("the child lies," "that child does everything he can to get out of being punished," "those children are always working deals behind my back"). Kohlberg's theory provides an impetus for teachers to stop, think and strategize before drawing conclusions.

Maslow's Theory of Human Motivation

The effective teacher wants to know what impacts his or her students thinking, feeling and reacting—those intrinsic conditions that exist and instill a student's desire to learn. Of all the theories I read about at the undergraduate level, Abraham Maslow's *Hierarchy of Needs* had the greatest impression on me. It made sense that certain needs must be satisfied and in place before kids (or adults, for that matter) can fully experience an advanced capacity to learn.

Maslow was trained as a behavioral psychologist, but became annoyed at the way behaviorists viewed human activity. In his opinion, their theories seemed limited, as they did not account for inherent human qualities. Maslow stated that people have an inner life and the potential for growth, creativity and free choice. While human beings are certainly subject to external events that shape them, they also have minds that develop from the inside out. According to Maslow, each person is born with a hierarchy of needs to be satisfied; these conditions exist in spite of environmental surroundings.

---

[4] *Ibid.*, 125.

Maslow identified six levels of needs, listed below from the most basic to the most advanced:

1. Physiological needs
2. Safety needs
3. Belongingness needs
4. Love needs
5. Self-esteem needs
6. Self-actualization needs

Fulfillment of one level of need sparks movement toward the next. Maslow's theory is not directly tied to a developmental continuum, nor is it limited to K–6 students; however, it does provide insight as to a student's capacity to learn.

If a child comes to school consistently hungry, tired, cold, anxious, or with a sense of hopelessness, learning is blocked. Children cannot learn in stressful chaos, nor are they open to embrace all that a teacher has to offer if they have not eaten. When basic needs are not fulfilled, the child is unable to progress forward despite a teacher's best efforts.

The informed educator asks, "What conditions exist for my students?" "How many children in my school are on free and reduced lunch?" "How do my students get to school?" "Where do they go after school?" "Are there systems in my school that help children feel a sense of belonging and compassion?" "In my teaching, do I attempt to balance positive statements well ahead of negative ones, thus building a child's esteem and sense of accomplishment?" All of these conditions affect the potential for learning.

Maslow's Theory and Its Impact on the Music Class

One of my part-time teaching posts included a population of children who lived, for the most part, in poverty. Over half of the student body received free and reduced lunch. Many waited anxiously outside the cafeteria doors every morning to eat breakfast. My 'classroom' was in the cafeteria, and I witnessed this scene on Mondays and Tuesdays, the days I taught there.

As I set up my corner of the large room, I watched children devour their breakfast; nothing else but eating was on their minds. On Mondays, the anxiousness of the students was far more obvious since many had not eaten a decent meal since Friday's school lunch.

Students would keep their coats on all day, even if the classroom was warm and cozy. They were anxious about losing the only coat they owned and the consequences weren't worth it. I witnessed how desperately they wanted to be noticed and be loved. The younger children would express that desire by clutching their teachers by the waist, while the intermediate kids were drawn to being a part of a clique or gang (in loose terms) with other students.

In this same school, I witnessed how educators can affect entire classrooms of children. One second-grade teacher was particularly gifted at taking her hungry, tired and somewhat-fearful group of seven year olds and transforming them into children who felt loved, who felt they belonged, and who would proudly boast of their accomplishments.

How did she do this? By satisfying their basic needs. There was always healthy food in her classroom, she was present at the door as they walked in, and she would issue the first hug of the day. Her students felt safe and protected in her presence.

This teacher's morning ritual included a welcome song and story time which included snippets of what the children were experiencing, thinking, had questions about, or were dreaming of. Math, science, language arts, and other academics did not start until she sensed all in the room were in a place where learning was possible. It was magical to watch her kids throughout the year as their self-esteem soared.

Her influence taught me to pay attention to who is walking into my music room. Children deserve adults who see them, welcome them, recognize what they might need, and provide the structure toward a safe and needs-filled environment.

Bloom's Taxonomy of Intellectual Behavior

Piaget and Kohlberg contributed to our understanding of human development while Maslow provided insight as to what intrinsically motivates learning to occur. Benjamin Bloom's theory is based on how learners process information.

Why is Bloom's Taxonomy included in a chapter on who's in the music class? While it could easily fit in Chapter 3 ("What's in the Music Class?"), it is linked more closely with the child as a person and how that person processes information.

Caine and Caine indicate that healthy children may "differ by as much as five years in their natural acquisition of basic skills."[5] Within a typical class of 25 students, children will

---

[5] Caine and Caine, 88.

demonstrate wide levels of comprehension. Bloom helps us sort out and classify those levels, thus giving insight as to what children are actually understanding.

According to Bloom and his associates, the levels of learning begin at basic knowledge and continue to a level where one is able to evaluate what he or she has learned. The theory is not linked to age or maturation. It is not a framework for studying the developmental level of a child. Rather, it provides categorical evidence of where children are in their basic understanding of issues and concepts. These levels, or stages, include (from lowest-level learning to highest):

- Knowledge stage
- Comprehension stage
- Application stage
- Analysis stage
- Synthesis stage
- Evaluation stage

Movement from one phase to the next comes at different times for different students. Effective educators know how to look for indicators that tell them in what level their learners are functioning. They use this information to structure teaching that inspires forward and upward movement. (It's yet another example of how and why master teachers pay close attention to their students).

Bloom's Taxonomy and Its Impact in the Music Class

Rather than tell of experiences that bear witness to his theory, a chart is provided to demonstrate how Bloom's Taxonomy might look within the general music curriculum. This chart can be closely aligned with Chapter 3, which deals with matters of curriculum. As such, the reader might wish to juxtapose this visual to Bruner's stages (found on page 50).

The chart below includes Bloom's six levels, intertwined with musical concepts to be learned, verbs that describe what the students are doing, and sample activities or questions that would trigger a learner to process information at a particular level.

Knowledge Level

Concepts	Verbs	Potential activities and questions
Time	Tell List	• Write a four-beat rhythm using quarter and eighth notes
Pitch	Describe Relate	• Just by looking at this melody, locate where the notes are highest
Structure	Locate	• Can you name the form, based on this visual?
Expressive Components	Write Find State	• Tell how the quiet section was created in the song we just heard
Style	Name	• List the different instruments you might find in a jazz combo

Comprehension Level

Concepts	Verbs	Potential activities and questions
Time	Explain	• Predict how this rhythm will sound when you play it on a drum
Pitch	Interpret Outline	• Compare the pitch of a soprano and alto voice. How do they differ?
Structure	Discuss Predict Restate	• Describe why this piece is an example of theme and variations
Expressive Components	Translate Compare	• Can you play an example of *crescendo/decrescendo*?
Style	Describe	• Compare the music of Bach and Berlioz. Who do you think needed a larger orchestra?

Application Level

Concepts	Verbs	Potential activities and questions
Time	Solve	• Show how you can rearrange this four-measure rhythm composition
Pitch	Show Use	• Use this set of notes, but arrange them in a way that makes them sound like a melody
Structure	Illustrate Construct	• Construct an AB piece, using you and your partner's composition ideas
Expressive Components	Complete Examine Classify	• Add *staccato* and *legato* to your melody and show how that would make it sound different
Style		• If you could ask Beethoven about his music, what questions would you include?

Analysis Level

Concepts	Verbs	Potential activities and questions
Time	Analyze Distinguish	• Identify where the bar lines need to be changed
Pitch	Examine	• Explain how this chord progression works
Structure	Compare Contrast Investigate	• Can you distinguish a rondo from ternary form?
Expressive Components	Categorize Identify	• Why do you think the composer increased the tempo?
Style	Explain Separate	• How is this music of Ghana linked to the dance we just learned?

Synthesis Level

Concepts	Verbs	Potential activities and questions
Time	Create Invent	• Compose a piece that has changing meter. What happens to the feel of the beat?
Pitch	Compose Predict	• How would this piece sound different if it were in minor rather than major?
Structure	Plan Construct	• What would happen if we included a coda rather than a D.C.?
Expressive Components	Design Imagine Propose	• Create a new way to illustrate a change in speed and volume
Style	Devise Formulate	• Propose a topic that might make an interesting idea for an opera

Evaluation Level

Concepts	Verbs	Potential activities and questions
Time	Judge	• Is there a better way to play that rhythm with a different instrument?
Pitch	Select Choose	• Do you think singing in a foreign language changes the way pitches work together?
Structure	Decide Justify Debate Verify	• Recommend to your partner how to create a B section that relates to, but is different than, his or her A section
Expressive Components	Argue Recommend Assess	• Conduct a song of your choice and evaluate how well you can show getting loud vs. getting soft
Style	Discuss	• Choose a composer and recommend him or her to your classmates. Be convincing.

Moving Toward 21st-Century Know-How

There is unlimited information to absorb regarding the teaching of children, with more information readily available every day. Effective educators draw on the theories and findings from the past while continuing to research current thoughts, practices and findings that will improve instruction and student understanding. Obviously, the more we know, the better our teaching will be.

Science and technology have advanced dramatically since the research era of Piaget, Kohlberg, Maslow, and Bloom (1920–70s). We have far more immediate access to information on what makes the brain and body work in human beings. The study of brain complexities is particularly astounding in its magnitude of findings.

As Caine and Caine explained:

> Educators do not need to be experts in brain anatomy, especially since even those who study the anatomical intricacies of brain functioning update their knowledge almost daily. However, what educators must have is some appreciation of how multifaceted the brain is in order to more fully appreciate the complexities involved in education.[6]

When I first began teaching, brain research (as it applied to education) was limited to discussions and articles on right brain/left brain and other fairly primitive ideas. We now know *so* much more. While scientific data continues to flow on the topic of brain research and its application for education, I've been increasingly interested in how specific aspects of brain research impacts children in the music class.

The "Triune" Brain

Educational psychologists who call themselves behaviorists primarily view people as products of their environment, while humanists see people as products of their inner desires and innate creativity. Current brain research blends the two and can be perceived as a simple algorithm: A (a unique brain) + B (a unique environment) = C (a unique brain organized on the basis of A + B).[7] Blending what is brought in with what exists

---

[6] *Ibid.*, 28.
[7] *Ibid.*, 32.

within occurs day-in and day-out, beginning from day one of life here on this earth.

Paul MacLean suggested that the human brain is actually three brains in one. All three impact how a person behaves, outwardly and inwardly, and how information is processed.[8] These three brains, from the most basic to the more advanced, are:

1. R-complex, also known as the Reptilian brain
2. Limbic System
3. Neocortex

The Reptilian brain consists largely of the brainstem and is related to physical survival and maintenance. It's the one we retreat to when we feel threatened and are contemplating fight or flight. One can see it triggered in an individual's physique and body position: the head goes down; the shoulders come forward; the face tenses. The image it strikes is like a snake coiling before it makes the decision to either leap forward to bite or slither away in retreat. The maintenance it provides helps with digesting food, breathing, chewing, swallowing—thing we do, but don't really think about. This particular brain prizes rituals, habits and actions that become automatic (get up, stretch and yawn, brush teeth). It's highly resistant to change (which is why bad habits are extremely difficult to alter).

The Limbic System includes two parts: the *amygdala* and the *hippocampus.* One section functions to associate events with emotion (the amygdala), while the other is linked to memory (hippocampus). This particular brain provides the first step in registering self-awareness, how we *feel* about things. It is associated and related to emotions. "The way children learn is through processing information through the Limbic System, sorting it out and tying to some level of emotion."[9]

The Limbic brain is activated and evident when we hear children say "I just *love* that song!" or "Ooh, I'm *really* good at this!" "Oh yeah… I remember that dance…" It's always fun to hear an entire group of kids go, "Yesssss!!" when it's announced they'll sing, play, dance to, or listen to one of their favorites. It's like a collective group of limbic systems making themselves known! These reactions show evidence that "emotions give a sense of reality to what we do and think and remember."[10]

---

[8] Paul MacLean, *The Triune Brain* (New York: Plenum Press, 1990).
[9] Caine and Caine, 63.
[10] *Ibid.*

The Neocortex is by far the largest of the three brains, taking up ⅚ of the space and encompassing the forehead, or frontal lobe. It makes language, speech, writing, creating, analyzing, sequencing, problem solving, and every other 'ing' associated with processing information in an advanced manner, possible. Scientists and medical researchers readily admit there are several unknowns about this part of the brain. Although its capacity is quite large, its function, in most humans, isn't fully used.

One of the primary reasons the Neocortex is not engaged as thoroughly as it could be is simply due to human nature. According to Caine and Caine, most people normally fall back on what they know, especially in times of stress. They call this process downshifting. It is a simple survival technique. I know I tend to drive the same routes and roads to 'play it safe', especially when travel time is limited. I tend to cook the same meals rather than explore a new recipe when company is coming. Humans tend to downshift rather than apply what the Neocortex can offer. We tend to rely on what has worked before, or worse yet, get frustrated and give up.

"Downshifting appears to affect many higher-order cognitive functions of the brain and thus can prevent us from learning and generating solutions for new problems. (It) is part of the reason students fail to apply higher levels of Bloom's Taxonomy."[11]

We see evidence of the Neocortex at work when students are actively engaged in the 'doing' of music: creating, composing, analyzing, applying symbol systems. We undoubtedly witness the downshifting process in classrooms, as well. When faced with limited time or resources, students hurry to finish a project or activity, relying on what they've known and done in the past rather than striving to solve the unknown. While practicing skills at a basic level is a good thing, consistent downshifting is not. The Neocortex allows profound learning to occur if given the time, setting, initiative, and support to be activated in lessons.

Students come to school with brains full of memory, emotion, and a perception of what the world is and what it isn't. Unless brain damaged, students have infinite possibilities for learning. While it's true that the mind is affected (positively and negatively) by home environment, educators must understand their role in providing the kind of environment and sup-

---

[11] *Ibid.*, 70.

port where advanced learning and problem solving can occur. We should remember the algorithm, A + B = C and be certain that we offer children a glimpse not only of what is possible, but what is also achievable.

Music educators tap into every level of thinking and feeling in each and every student. A music specialist watches a child grow and develop, moving from one Piagetian cognitive level to the next, exhibiting decisions that form the basis of what he or she believes about trust and loyalty (Kohlberg), and processing information from simple to profound levels of understanding (Maslow and Bloom).

An effective music educator marvels at student's thinking and abilities. Eph Ehly wrote, "Because music reflects every aspect of life, the one who teaches it should have an appreciation for every aspect of life."[12]

Appreciating every aspect of life is a tall order. Appreciating every child, however, is quite do-able. Accepting who the children are, with their diversity and exceptionalities, should be an assumed predisposition for teachers. The more information we have for understanding how our students think, feel, process information, and progress in understanding, the deeper that appreciation can be.

Special-Needs Students

Within our schools, we have children who function and process in multiple ways. Part of this is due to culture and background, while much of it comes from how brains and bodies translate information. All learners are not the same, particularly in today's typical classroom. Of the many models seen in public school classrooms throughout the country, there is one 'for sure'—educators *will* have special needs students within their classes.

There is a *Peanuts* cartoon that shows Charlie Brown and Lucy chatting over philosophical matters. Lucy asks Charlie Brown if he's ever noticed how people on cruise ships decide which way to face their deck chairs: Some people face their chairs toward the back of the ship, to see where they've been, while others face them forward, to see where they're going. Lucy asks, "Charlie Brown, on the cruise ship of life, which

---

[12] Ehly, 187.

way is your deck chair facing?" Charlie Brown grimly replies, "I don't know. I've never been able to get one unfolded."

Sometimes what seems simple to most of us is incredibly challenging to others. Students receiving special-needs services may find specific areas of instruction a challenge, but they are to be appreciated, celebrated and considered entitled learners within the music classroom.

According to the National Education Association (NEA), in 2005 over 6,000,000 public school students are provided special-education services. This number has increased well over 33% in the past ten years. Within my school of 500 plus students, approximately 22% receive some level of special service. This increase has occurred in extremely rapid succession considering the relative newness of it: "Only four decades ago, those currently enrolled in special education would have been isolated in separate institutions or simply kept at home, with little or no chance of ever becoming independent, productive, citizens."[13]

The NEA and Department of Education indicate special-education support is provided for students with one or more of the following:

- Speech and language difficulty
- Motor challenges
- Developmental delays
- Learning disabilities
- Health impairments
- Emotional or behavioral issues
- Orthopedic impairments
- Mental retardation
- Multiple disabilities
- Hearing impairment/Deafness
- Visual impairment/Blindness
- Autism
- Traumatic brain injury

This list has grown tremendously since the early 1980s, when I entered music education as a teacher. Our perception and acceptance of 'special learners' has certainly come a long way since then.

---

[13] NEA, Special Education/IDEA

Laws, Legislation and Logistics

When I first began to teach, Public Law 94-142, entitling education for all students, was fairly new. Ratification of the law in 1975 prompted a surge of legislative action and entitlements for this particular population. States and districts across the country were expected to provide students with the services and resources they required to gain a full and balanced education.

I have to admit, I had *very* limited interactions with anyone who appeared 'differently abled' when I attended K–12 school and college. I took a methods course in the education building during my undergraduate studies that included basic information about PL 94-142. I passed the final test, indicating that I understood what the law meant. Obviously, my combined lack of teaching *and* life experiences with special-education students diminished any meaningful instruction I might offer, particularly those first few years.

The summer prior to my first year of teaching, my school was asked to house the "trainable mentally handicapped" (as they were labelled) students living in the district. These students were chronologically aged 5–22 while developmentally aged 1 year to about 5. Some were verbal, some were not. Some were born with the disability while others suffered traumatic head injury or extreme illness as young children.

The students were divided into a primary group and an intermediate group. The division was based on chronological age only. It was very strange to be a 22-year-old instructor teaching students who were 21. To the eye, most would be described as young men and women. Cognitively, however, their brains operated at a pre-operational stage.

At first, I was uncomfortable. As mentioned, I'd never been around students like this. Not only was teaching still relatively uncomfortable, but it seemed unusual to be teaching students who were so unfamiliar to me. My first year of teaching was the ultimate learning curve in *so* many ways!

What I didn't grasp at the time was that the whole nation was undergoing a huge learning curve, educationally. Thank goodness we have advanced our skills and systems for helping *all* students succeed in our schools. The presence of special-education students is no longer an oddity, and educators now have unlimited resources to utilize in order to provide the best education possible for their students.

After PL 94-142, legislation continued at a rapid pace with the more significant signing, in 1990, of the "Individuals with Disabilities Education Act" (IDEA). This law was updated in 1997 and again in 2004, expanding specifics to include language regarding access, discipline and assessment as it relates to "No Child Left Behind" (NCLB). While there are many political conversations referring to the NCLB legislation, educators agree that the progress made with special-education students is, for the most part, in a positive direction.

Music education for special-needs children is *not* music therapy. The intent and design of interventions (not instruction) in music therapy settings, as stated by the American Music Therapy Association, are designated to "promote wellness, manage stress, alleviate pain, express feelings, enhance memory, improve communication, and promote physical rehabilitation."[14] There are times when a special-education teacher might request a specific song or movement activity or listening selection to be utilized due to its nonmusical pay-offs—that's not the issue. The root of what music educators do comes back to music *instruction*. The events and nonmusical pay-offs will always occur if the environment for musical learning is presented in a manner conducive to the emotional level of the students.

MENC: The National Association of Music Education published standards for elementary and junior high school and included statements regarding music instruction for students with special needs. These are excellent guidelines to consider as well as implement.

- When students with disabilities are included in regular music classes, their placement is determined on the same basis as placement for students without disabilities.
- Music educators are involved in placement decisions and are fully informed about the needs of each student.
- Music instruction is provided for students receiving special education who are not included in regular music classes.
- Music instruction for students with disabilities is designed to teach practical music skills and knowledge that will assist the students in functioning successfully in the music environments of home, school and community.

---

[14] For more information, visit www.musictherapy.org.

- Students with disabilities are given the same opportunities to elect choral/instrumental instruction as other students; if a music task cannot be performed by students with disabilities, adaptation will be provided.[15]

Regardless of classroom configuration or where/how services are delivered, it is clear that effective music educators play a role in fulfilling the educational plan for the special-needs child. This plan is often referred to as the student's IEP, or Individualized Education Plan.

In some states and districts, the IEP is written and evaluated by a team of teachers. In others, it is completed with those teachers immediately providing a 'service' to the individual student. Either model works, as long as the music teacher gains enough basic information to best instruct children who have different ways of processing information. New teachers are strongly advised to learn the extent of their district's privacy issues in order to behave in an ethical and professional manner, if and when students are discussed.

Special Learners in the Music Classroom: Teacher/Student Expectations

Do special-needs children affect the learning environment? All classrooms are fundamentally based on the child and the teacher and the relationship they build. This fact does not change according to who's in the room. Positive educators create community with their students. A teacher perceives the job as one human interacting with another in a manner that stimulates learning, builds confidence, and expands experiences to last a lifetime.

Special needs or not, students have the right to expect their music teachers to see them as capable individuals. Anything less would be demeaning to our profession. This leads to some philosophical thoughts of mine regarding special-education students and their place in the music class:

---

[15] From *National Standards for Arts Education.* © 1994 by Music Educators National Conference (MENC). Used by permission. The complete National Arts Standards and additional materials relating to the Standards are available from MENC—The National Association for Music Education, 1806 Robert Fulton Drive, Reston, VA 20191.

1. Regardless of disability or limitation, students will be treated in a respectful and age-appropriate manner.

This implies that students in the class who are 21 on the outside but four on the inside shouldn't be reduced to singing songs intended for four-year-old children. The music teacher must respect the chronological age of the student when selecting materials for listening, singing or movement.

2. Music teachers have the right to request and expect assistance when a special-needs student integrates into the classroom and receives assistance in every other aspect of their day.

If the IEP for a particular student calls for a full-time aide, then the aide should accompany the special-needs child to music class. If the presence of an aide helps the student learn and function more productively in other settings, then the music teacher will welcome the adult assistant.

3. Special-education teachers have the right to expect dialogue and professional interactions with the music educator.

While there may be specifics regarding a child that cannot be shared, both professionals need to fundamentally believe that they share the student's best interests and best education in their hearts and minds and base their discussions around this goal.

4. Special needs students—all of them, regardless of limitations—can learn.

It's up to the teacher to find the best way possible to capitalize on what children can do and to make adjustments so that musical growth can occur. Music teachers are professionally obligated to learn who the child is, what the child is capable of, and to celebrate his or her accomplishments.

5. All children, regardless of cognitive, physical, emotional, or behavioral issues, draw strength from routine, rituals and a positive environment.

Maintain a classroom atmosphere where rituals and routines are established and practiced (see Chapter 4 for specifics) and high expectations are held.

6. Appreciate students for who they are.

Appreciate the opportunity to teach them as well.

Teaching special-education students requires skilled instruction, informed practice and honest answers to self:

1. What do I believe about learners, especially those who are outside 'the norm'?
2. How do I prioritize what I teach and how I teach to include all of the students I'll meet?
3. What do I believe music class has to offer *all* students?
4. What do I need to know about *who* the students are to be as effective as possible with everyone I teach?
5. What do students see and hear when they come to my class?
6. What kind of climate do I consistently maintain? Is each child welcomed into my classroom?
7. Do I believe music belongs in everyone's educational 'package'?
8. How do I believe musical growth is measured?
9. Can I learn to measure musical accomplishment in a variety of ways?
10. Do I consider myself part of an instructional team designed to help a student accomplish all that is possible?

Who's in the music classroom? Students with brains, hearts, ambitions, struggles, abilities, and potential. I believe the more we embrace this attitude as the best descriptor of our children, the clearer the road toward effective instruction. In the end, we are not merely teaching music to people, we are teaching *people* through music.

What's Inside the Music Classroom?

Inside the music class, there's a teacher (novice, new or experienced), there are students (diverse in their learning systems, styles and developmental levels), and there is an instructional setting (the classroom structure or, in some cases, the lack of one) where one can observe the workings of a qualified instructor. What does that look like? What does it include?

Effective teachers establish a relationship with students to create an atmosphere for learning. In addition, they organize the content of music—the subject itself—to be taught in ways that generate integrity and purpose for its place in our schools. Selecting *what* will be taught, *when* it will be taught, and *how* it will be taught is vital to the success of any music program. The right instructional system in the hands of an effective teacher blends the art and heart in careful balance.

Many resources are available to consult on the topic of curriculum and methodology in the elementary general music setting. The purpose of this chapter is to look at basic frameworks of music instruction and to encourage the reader to ponder organized systems for his or her delivery in the classroom.

Amongst the information on curriculum development and learning strategies are philosophical inquiry and attention to the individual teacher. I've found that teachers spend instructional time on that which they believe to be valuable: what is deemed valuable stems from one's philosophical beliefs. This chapter asks the reader to consider articulating what those beliefs are while designing or selecting curriculum.

It's difficult to fully embrace what one is to teach without a foundation of *why* it should be taught. I have no doubt that music has a place in every child's education. My belief is based on the following tenets: Like all subject areas, music has a theory (symbolic system), content (the essence of what is attributed to the subject area), skills to be developed (unique to the subject area), pedagogy (often framed in "how others do it"), and historical data and documentation. Properly taught, music is a subject area that is filled with rigor and academic structure, as well as wonder and awe. It parallels science and math, but in unique perspectives.

While science and math exist to explain the world, music and art exist to *express* the world. Science and math attempt to define what is; music and art attempt to *describe* the human reaction to what is seen, felt and dreamt about. Music, as a school subject, has a profound place in the education of all children. It is a music educator's job to make that visible and obvious.

The Content of Music Instruction

What exactly is included in any standard music curriculum? What concepts are found in music that set it apart from other subject areas? Regardless of approach, pedagogy or grade level, music content includes the following broad set of basic concepts:

Time	Rhythm; beat; meter
Pitch	Frequency—high/low, melody, clef reference, tonality
Structure	Repetition/contrast; pattern; phrase
Style	Musically and historically grounded
Expressive Components	Tempo; dynamics; articulation
Timbre	Instrumentation; settings; production sources

Within each of these basics exist a myriad of mini-concepts that are included in a solid music-education curricula. These 'feeder concepts' drive the step-by-step instructional process and provide the framework for sequential learning.

For example, let's consider the concept of time and one of its primary feeders, rhythm. All would agree that rhythm is a key component of music instruction, but its purpose in music is to establish units of duration in time—long sounds, short sounds, and silences. If we consider the teaching and understanding of rhythm in a step-by-step sequence, the breakdown might look like this:

Rhythm

What is it?

Sounds organized into patterns of longer sounds, shorter sounds and silences.

What can it look like?

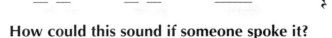

How could this sound if someone spoke it?

Long,	Long,	Short-short,	Long,
Short-short,	Short-short,	Long,	(Shh!)

How would it look in regular music notes?

Is there a formal way I can organize these notes?

What can I do with these notes once I understand how they sound as well as how they function?

- Rearrange them
- Speak them
- Clap them
- Walk them
- Sing them
- Play them on an instrument
- Speed them up
- Slow them down
- Add more
- Change the longs and shorts to real words

I can also…

- Write two different patterns and have my buddy speak one while I speak the other
- Start reading them very softly and gradually get louder
- Read them with my buddy, but have each of us start at different times
- Make some of the longs very smooth and the shorts very choppy

A lesson plan calling for the instruction of rhythm continues through the tenure of a child's elementary experience. As a primary feeder to the concept of time, rhythmic activity is demonstrated through multiple skills. In the list of options on the facing page, students are singing, listening, creating, composing, writing, reading, playing instruments, and moving. They are constantly showing, in a proactive manner, their understanding of the concept rhythm. Music learning occurs as a result of participation. Passivity is not an option in music class!

A music lesson at the elementary level engages learners in ways that lead students toward the understanding and application of basic content. This content is normally couched in curriculum guides available in multiple resources.

Beyond Content and Skills—Published Curricula

Selecting the curriculum on which to rely can become overwhelming since there are multiple, as well as excellent, supportive resources. I do recommend that new teachers investigate what is readily available once hired by a particular district:

- Is there a district-published framework?
- Is there a district-wide curricula or adoption purchased for every building?
- Does the state have published documents regarding music curricula and what benchmarks? (Each geographical area seems to have its own labels or titles for these; in my district, we have frameworks and GLEs (Grade Level Expectations). In the state of Washington, we have state frameworks and EALRs (Essential Academic Learning Requirements).
- Does the school have an adopted Basel series that is considered the framework for what is taught and learned? (These curriculum guides are written and organized by grade level and are quite extensive and inclusive in lesson variety and supportive materials. They are especially helpful for the beginning general music teacher.)

Establishing Priorities for Instructional Goals

Beyond published documents, whether district based, state produced, or published by a national company, a teacher must establish the nitty-gritty of instruction based on a variety of variables. Among these are the diverse population of students, the frequency and amount of instructional time, the resources and materials available, prior music instruction (for the students), and community and district expectations.

I advise developing a few simple priorities to serve as guides when considering lessons and units. These priorities should reflect what the students should know and be able to do when they leave the school. They are best if they naturally and comfortably reflect your belief system and what you will refer to when making instructional decisions. Instructional priorities should align with each student's capabilities, regardless of physical or cognitive limitations, as well as abide with the teacher's individual strengths. I believe we teach best what we best know how to do.

I have three priorities. They are simple, but have proven to be effective and purposeful for my use. They align with my philosophy of elementary music education's purpose in our schools; they also are an outgrowth of the instructional strengths I perceive are my skills as a teacher:

Patty's Pretty Simple Priorities

- Each student will understand what he can do, independent of the teacher, to improve the quality and character of his singing voice. (I can't make a student consistently *apply* these things, but I can be sure to include lessons that build these habits and create the vocabulary for improved singing).
- Each student will have a *minimum* of one successful and memorable experience playing an instrument. (Recently, I had a twelfth grader come to visit and recall with delight playing the triangle at a performance as a third grader. He remembered the song, the setting and the audience's positive reaction.)
- Each student will have a general sense of musical styles. (In the past, I used the scenario of going into a CD store—would a student have enough information to know what she might find in the jazz section as opposed to the ethnic section as opposed to the classical section? Now I use the iTunes radio and store in this scenario, as students don't go to CD stores too often anymore.)

These priorities guide my steps as I consult and apply published curricula and frameworks existing in my school or district. Furthermore, I develop my own lessons that align with and progress toward these goals. Finally, and most importantly, these priorities are inclusive and keep me focused on what is attainable for each student in my school. (Diverse populations exist everywhere. See Chapter 2 for more details on this topic.)

Breaking Instruction into Practical Pieces à la Bruner

Once a music teacher enters the classroom, he or she has frameworks for what is to be taught (curriculum), has established priorities for setting instructional goals, and has multiple skills to build and reinforce. Now it's time to establish the remainder of the picture: the *how and when* of curricular options.

Dr. Jerome Bruner wrote that children are capable of learning anything at any time if presented in a sequential and developmentally appropriate manner. He suggested that, in all learning, children engage in a three-stage continuum toward understanding concepts. Each stage lays the foundation for the next.[1]

Stage 1 is *enactive* in design. Students engage in learning through *active* involvement. For example, in order to under-stand what a dog is, a child pets a dog, observes how it moves, watches it eat, understands the nature of its tail, etc. In the en-active stage in the music class, children are singing, listening, moving; they are engaged in music activities before labeling concepts occurs.

Enactive learning exists at any age and for anything to be learned. It is a vital step toward understanding. It's hard to imagine how scary the roads would be if young drivers didn't actively engage in driving prior to getting a license. Eating at a restaurant where the chef has not actively engaged in mixing ingredients would be a risky endeavor as well.

Certainly, enactive involvement in music learning is a vital stage for a student's understanding, regardless of age or grade level. Through active participation, teachers can observe and assess students' general response to music at the root level. If a student has trouble perceiving tempo changes, it will be obvious in his movement. The teacher would provide further experiences in this area before assessing steady beat. Likewise, if a child experiences difficulty altering pitches in her singing voice, this would not be the time to assess her ability to sing a major scale.

Once the student has demonstrated, through his actions, that he is progressing, the next step is introduced. Bruner calls this the *iconic stage*. An icon is a pictorial or physical image or reflection of something. Back to the dog analogy. A child can look at a picture of a dog, the image only, and will be re-minded how the dog felt, how he pet it, etc. Young children often relive a sensation when looking at picture books: they'll run their hand through the air, "petting" the imaginary dog; they'll 'kiss' the baby and they'll 'smell' the flower. Likewise, a beginning cook relies on pictures to have an image of what a particular dish is supposed to look like once it's out of the oven and ready to serve.

---

[1] Jerome Bruner, *The Culture of Education* (Cambridge, MA: Harvard University Press, 1994).

Earlier in this chapter, I showed a sequence of rhythmic instruction and included the following iconic representation of a rhythmic pattern:

I teach rhythm reading using icons like these. I'll ask the students what they see, and they'll normally reply "long lines and short lines" or "dashes." It's easy for them to say "long" as I trace my finger along the long line, and "short-short," as my finger goes under the short lines. (A quarter rest can look like anything, since it's silent. I just go ahead and draw a real quarter rest, asking the kids to silently feel the beat when my finger goes under it.) In less than 30 seconds, young students are reading rhythms. Better yet, they can relate the rhythms to a warm-up movement activity, a listening selection or a song learned.

Every concept in music has iconic possibilities. Much of what children experience in their regular classrooms relate directly to this experience. Kids learn ABA and other patterns in their kindergarten classes by viewing shapes or colors (icons for form). Students track highs and lows, ups and downs, when learning to write letters. Following a melodic contour icon is simple and clear—the skill is well grounded from preschool forward.

When I introduce a more complex concept, say unison vs. two-part harmony, with older kids, I first engage them in singing, listening, physical movement, etc., then draw their attention to a visual that might look something like this:

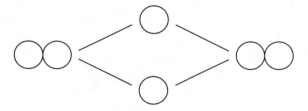

I'll ask the students to describe what they see and how the image relates to a prior activity. The answers are usually quite articulate: "Well, we all started on the same note. Then half of us went lower in pitch, while the other half went higher, and then we came back to singing/playing the same note."

Within the grades I teach, a vast majority of my students' instructional time is spent in the enactive and iconic stages, so

that when they begin using the next stage, the *symbolic system*, it is no mystery. The lines and spaces with notes and rhythms make perfect sense; no rote instruction or memorization is required. It's a natural passage from one stage to the next when everything is presented logically and in a manner appropriate to the learners.

In order to fully understand how each of Bruner's stages progress, let's return to the dog analogy. Person A sees a dog, pets a dog, observes the dog do 'dog things', and now has a general understanding of a dog. Later, Person A looks at books and sees a bright cover indicating pictures of dog breeds. He picks up this book, and says, "Ah yes, that's the dog I saw. It was a beagle." Finally, Person A would like to have a pet of his own. He calls the Humane Society and asks if they have any beagles. He knows a lot about beagles. He also knows that a poodle will not do. Although he's not seen a poodle in person, he has read a description of a poodle's temperament in a dog book. Person A can apply an overriding symbolic system to the notion of a dog without the enactive and iconic steps necessary. The result? Person A gets his beagle and is now a happy pet owner.

The budding chef can eventually predict the outcome of a meal by reading the ingredients and recipe—no pictures necessary for the experienced cook. A scientist no longer must mix salt with water to understand what $NaCl$ and H_2O will get her. The musician can translate long lines to quarter notes, short lines to eighth notes, and still understand the duration of each sound as they relate in time. He can hear how it will sound long before it's counted out loud or played on an instrument.

I follow Bruner's stages to teach every concept. Rhythmic independence, for instance, is taught through enactive involvement, iconic representation and, finally, symbolic reading. I help my students make the transition from icon to symbols by placing notes over the icons for several lessons:

As they become more comfortable with the symbols themselves, I move students from saying "long, long, short-short, long" to "1 2 3& 4." (I've found using numbers for counting is a natural step toward understanding meter and the purpose of barlines. It is also the preferred technique used by the secondary level ensemble programs in our district.) Eventually, the icons are no longer needed; the students can interpret the symbols on their own.

Our goal as teachers should be to provide students with the tools they need to manipulate, create and make music on their own. Not everyone will become a composer, but all students in music class should grow in their ability to utilize music's basic symbolic and theoretical systems. While in-depth study and understanding of notation may not be in all of my students' grasps, demystifying those 'black dots with lines attached' is a relatively easy step to include.

Let's return to articulating priorities. I know several excellent music teachers who include some level of music literacy as one of their top priorities for students. While I believe in the sequential instruction of music's symbolic system (so that the theory and mechanisms of music can be used by the student), I do not support music notation being taught separately from other logically sequential concepts. Memorizing where a G is on the staff means little when that's all a student has been told.

Understanding how symbolic music notation works allows us to interpret what other musicians/composers create. Likewise, it gives the student the ability to communicate his or her musical ideas in a manner so that other music readers, anywhere, can replay them. That's the power of understanding the symbolic system. I believe that applying notation in a personally authentic manner (either reading and performing, or composing and creating) makes music notation meaningful and full of purpose.

It's up to each teacher to decide on what to spend instuctional time. If developing music literacy is a vital priority, I recommend teaching it within a process and sequence that makes sense to the students and fits one's instructional style. The goal is to advance what students know and are able to do while bringing personal satisfaction to the forefront.

As Pagel and Spevacek noted, "Teaching is an ego-less profession. One where your main goal is to not only pass on all of your knowledge to your students, but also to see that your students take that knowledge to the next level to become even more successful than you."[2]

The 'Been There/Done That' System

How can music-reading skills be sharpened? The symbolic system is primed to appear when students have experienced rhythm, pitch, form, expression, style, and timbre through enactive experiences and have begun utilizing icons to show what they know and interpret what they've done. It arrives with ease and comfort; students know it is not an unusual language or code known only to talented musicians. Melodic and rhythmic reading and interpretation is actually fun for the students, since it taps into what they already know how to do and have done since preschool—recognize patterns. My approach for employing pattern recognition and recall is referred to as the 'been there/done that' system (for lack of a more scholarly title).

Here's how it works. Let's assume fourth-grade students are playing the soprano recorder. They've each learned to apply and describe how to maintain a quality tone; they've added fingers and taken away fingers and know that results in the

---

[2] Randy Pagel and Linda Spevacek, *The Choral Director's Guide to Sanity...and Success!* (Dayton, OH: Heritage Music Press, 2004) 24.

pitch going up or down. The students have echoed simple phrases from me, and from each other, in a partner activity (enactive participation). They've learned to call one particular sound a B when the top hole and the thumb hole are covered. Likewise, the class has learned adding more fingers results in lower notes, A, and G. They've followed a visual of a three-note melody that has the letters B, A, and G similar to the one below (iconic stage):

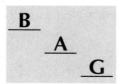

The fourth graders rewrite the icon to show repeated notes, skipped notes, etc., making up their own simple three-note patterns:

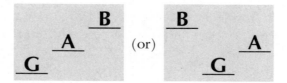

We hear the students play these patterns and watch their eyes follow the icon visual with ease. Eventually, we are convinced they are ready to make the shift to the symbols on the staff. Altogether, we have:

1. Heard the students play the instrument
2. Assessed their ability to control the sound
3. Watched them move from one pitch to the next
4. Followed their eyes as they play a visualization of a three-note melody

Now they are ready for step 5,

5. Interpret pitches and rhythms on a musical staff

Simple!

We start with identifying the first three notes. Through experience with these three pitches, the students know they are B, A and G:

Once that's accomplished, the remainder of the notes are drawn from looking back to previous pitches identified—'been there, done that'. Likewise, if a four-measure melody is written, we'll use the same system to identify repeated phrases or measures, contour, sequence, individual pitches, etc.

What happens? Students begin to *predict* what the four measures will sound like before they are played. The students know how to look for patterns—a skill they've practiced multiple times in a variety of settings—and apply them to making music on their own. It's a gratifying accomplishment students experience and will remember. The students understand how music notation is conceived, and how it relates to the actual sound. It makes sense to the learners because it is logical. It results in students having the tools to progress toward advanced levels of musicianship. Beyond that, it's personally meaningful.

Student Learning Systems

We have our concepts (time, pitch, structure, style, expressive components, timbre), a variety of musical skills (singing, playing, moving, listening, reading, improvising, conducting, creating, composing, writing, etc.), and a system of organizing sequential steps toward learning (enactive, iconic, symbolic). Another essential step to consider is the students' natural learning systems—the manner in which learning takes place.

In her book, *Teaching to the Brain's Natural Learning Systems*, Barbara K. Given describes five identifiable systems that are engaged when people learn. According to Given, each of these systems, outlined below, enable, allow, encourage, and otherwise facilitate students' ability 'to':

Emotional Learning System: the need to be me
- Develop relationships, trust, feelings of safety
- Open up and learn
- Have a passion toward learning

Social Learning System: the need to belong
- Be a part of a group, identify with others
- Work with cultural norms
- Develop a sense of connectiveness with others

Physical Learning System: the need to do
- Know what it feels like
- Show what is known (response)
- Develop habits of learning strengthened by bodily reactions

Cognitive Learning System: the need to know
- Understand and process information
- Make sense of new learning
- Understand the 'what' and 'how' of things

Reflective Learning System: the need to experiment and explore
- Understand the if-then effect, scientific inquiry
- Exercise a uniquely human trait to satisfy curiosity[3]

According to Given, "Emotional, social, physical systems tend to be the most powerful in terms of their demands. The level of their functioning determines how effectively the cognitive and reflective systems operate."[4]

The good news? When we consider music instruction and music as an academic, its heart and soul live in the emotional, social and physical systems. While it's true the other two systems are engaged during music instruction, students have the emotional, social and physical systems dramatically engaged in *effective* music classrooms. The normal range of activities in an elementary general music class triggers the brain toward deeper levels of thinking. I've had classroom teachers tell me their students are able to concentrate and focus better in math

---

[3] Barbara K. Given, *Teaching to the Brain's Natural Learning Systems* (Alexandria, VA: Association for Supervision and Curriculum Development, 2002).

[4] *Ibid.*, 129.

when it occurs after music class. The instructional atmosphere of music class stimulates the mind's cognitive and reflective learning in more profound ways.

Provided an atmosphere where all five learning systems are engaged, the music class will naturally include opportunities for students to:

- *Describe* what they see, hear, play
- *Create* music through improvised or structured stages
- *Respond* to music through kinesthetic and aesthetic means
- *Perform* music to demonstrate multiple levels of understanding

These four processes—describing, creating, responding, and performing—encompass all aspects of music learning and should be considered when putting together lesson plans.

Putting It All Together

We now have a composite picture of what constitutes the framework of a music curriculum:

- The articulation of priorities and goals
- The inclusion of concepts and skills
- The adherence to learning sequence and systems
- The engagement of students in describing, creating and performing

The flow chart on the following page illustrates how all of these steps move from one phase to the next, with learning as the goal.

Teacher Priorities and Goals

Music Concepts	**Music Skills**
Time	Singing
Pitch	Playing
Structure	Moving
Style	Listening
Expressive Components	Reading
Timbre	Writing

Learning Sequence

Enactive
Iconic
Symbolic

Learning Systems

Emotional
Social
Physical
Cognitive
Reflective

Describes Music
Creates Music
Responds to Music
Performs Music

We get it!
We understand!

Final result? Students who can demonstrate and apply their understanding in ways that make it personal, memorable and significant. Teachers begin with goals and priorities for the students and end with students demonstrating understanding in ways that are joy-filled.

There is tremendous gratification felt when a teacher watches his or her students participate with their hearts, minds and bodies. That's when teaching is truly a human and meaningful experience.

Methodologies

It's impossible to enter the world of the general music teacher without reading or hearing the names Orff, Kodály, Dalcroze, and Gordon. In the United States, these particular names generally refer to methods of teaching: they represent approaches one might employ to teach the very same concepts addressed earlier in this chapter. Each of these particular methods is supported by professional affiliations (at the state, regional, and/or national level) and publishes informative journals. In addition, they support workshops and trainings throughout the country for continuing education credit.

While each method has unique strengths and attributes, they do remain a method—a 'how to' rather than a 'what to'. Fundamentally, student understanding is gained from a teacher of music who can organize instruction in a sequential and developmentally appropriate manner. The teacher has the prerogative to select one method or another to accomplish this task; however, utilizing any one of these systems provides a means to an end. The end remains the knowledge and ability to apply musical concepts in ways that have meaning for students.

It may be a pet peeve of mine, but I really don't understand when elementary music teachers indicate they teach Orff or Kodály. What does that mean? Perhaps if the response was, "I teach music to children and the method I use was created and adapted for general music instruction by a German composer and educator named Carl Orff" or "I teach music to students and utilize a theory of instruction called Kodály. Kodály was a Hungarian composer who was concerned about the integrity of music instruction," I might react differently.

Bottom line? I'm a proud eclectic. It doesn't mean I skate around the curriculum without a system of instruction; rather, it simply means I've not chosen to become a purist in any one methodology. Each approach has contributed to my professional repertoire of things to do, but I've elected to keep my overall instruction true to who I am and to use the variety of strengths I bring to teaching.

Don't get me wrong—adhering to one specific methodology is not a negative aspiration! Some of my favorite teacher friends are purists, in one method or the other, and are exceptionally effective at what they do. They are that way, however, with or without the method. They've developed strengths *as a teacher*. As an added bonus, they've developed skills in applying a specific approach to instruction in a way that makes sense to them and their students.

It's up to you to select how best to teach your students, based on multiple variables. Depending on your strengths and passions, one approach may be a better fit than another. Regardless of methodology, the 'what' of music instruction will always consist of concepts and skills, while the 'how' is based on the best way an individual teacher passes on knowledge. I believe it's in a teacher's best interest to know the general tenets and beliefs of each method—after all, they are part of the fabric of our profession.

Selecting a method should be each teacher's choice, however, a particular method may be required of all music teachers in a particular district. For instance, in Washington, some districts require completion of Level I of the Orff-Schulwerk methodology in order to maintain employment there. There are regions of the country that are known for their affinity to one methodology or another.

I suggest that new teachers take advantage of the workshops available sponsored by the state, regional and national organizations of the Orff method (American Orff-Schulwerk Association, www.aosa.org), the Kodály method (Organization of American Kodály Educators, www.oake.org), the Dalcroze method (Dalcroze Society of America, www.dalcrozeusa.org), and the Gordon Method (Gordon's Institute of Music Learning, www.giml.org). These workshops provide a wonderful way to get ideas for lessons, as well as network with fellow music educators. They are an informative—and fun—way to spend the weekend or a couple of weeks in the summer.

For further information, I urge the reader to consult the excellent summary and comparison of these methods in *Music in Childhood,* by Campbell and Scott-Kassner. They include an excellent chart for comparing and contrasting the methods above, plus CMP (Comprehensive Musicianship Project),

MMCP (Manhattanville Music Curriculum Project), ETM (Education Through Music), and the Phyllis Weikart system through movement education.

As Campbell and Scott-Kassner wrote, "Despite the myriad of techniques intended to advance the musical development of children, each teacher in the end chooses to incorporate pedagogical aspects that are harmonious with his personal goals and definitions of music education."[5]

Planning 101—How Do I Start?

In the month of August I go to my school and retrieve a blank plan book from our workroom. (It's very exciting, even if I have done it repeatedly year after year!) The first thing I do with this blank plan book is write my name and the school years on the cover. Then, I sit with a pen and calendar and place the dates of every single week, for 38 weeks. All holidays and non-student days are noted. The last 'nonlesson' thing I add is the schedule, class-by-class, day-by-day and week-by-week.

This ritual triggers the start of a brand new year for me. The organizational structure is in place before one word is written that would come close to looking like a lesson plan. I find comfort in this activity—it signals renewal.

The final steps are to ask myself, "What will I do the first day? What will they do the first week? When should they be able to demonstrate what they've learned?" Thus begins the art of planning.

Lesson planning is like a map in that it should help you and the students get where you want to go. The intent of any lesson plan is to provide direction to and documentation of a goal. All lesson plans have common traits: who is involved; what concept and skills will be taught; what the students will do; how understanding will be assessed; which materials will be required; etc.

Normally, student teachers arrive at my school with excellent templates to help guide lesson planning. In an attempt to help my interns think more thoroughly and deeply through a lesson, I give them the option of using a longer list of 'ingredients' to consider. It embraces a bit more of the nitty-gritty to lesson planning. It includes the following:

---

[5] Patricia Shehan Campbell and Carol Scott-Kassner, *Music in Childhood: From Preschool through the Elementary Grades* (New York: Schirmer Books, 1995) 68.

Music Lesson Flow Chart

Who's involved?

Particular class:
Grade level:
Distinguishing personality traits (of the class):

What do the students need to know how to do before beginning this lesson?

Learning characteristics?
Behavioral tendencies?
Skills?

What materials/resources need to be set before the lesson begins?

Visual references:
Audio:
Instruments located and ready for distribution:
Additional (mallets, chairs, etc.):
Papers and/or hand-outs and/or books:

On what musical concepts will you concentrate?

Pitch:
Time:
Structure:
Expressive Components
Timbre:
Style:

What stage(s) will the students experience through this lesson?

Enactive (what kind and level of participation?)
Iconic (what visuals? Ones you've drawn or they've drawn?)
Symbolic

What skills will the students experience and demonstrate?

Singing:
Listening:
Instrument playing:
Moving:
Reading music:
Notating music:
Improvising:

Will the students experience a lesson that encompasses multiple learning systems?
Emotional:
Social:
Physical:
Cognitive:
Reflective:

What kind of space will the students require? Where will they be?
Room setup:
Student placement:

What will the students show or do to demonstrate understanding?
Activities, written or drawn documentation, self-evaluation, other?

In addition to this particular form, I ask student teachers to begin to establish rituals and routines that give the students an instructional foundation. One of the rituals student interns observe in my classroom occurs when the students walk through the door.

Students enter: I meet and greet. They sit in 'circle spots' and become involved in a series of rhythm-building and beat-

building exercises. They echo pitches together and/or individually and review a song or dance before launching into the primary concept(s) of the lesson. This routine occurs almost everyday in my music room. Students expect it and find comfort in its familiarity. One would think they'd tire of starting things the same way, but if I throw in something different, the younger children almost always ask, "But, what about our warm-ups?"

The other lesson 'rule' I strongly urge student teachers, interns, and mentees to pay attention to is their interaction with the students. It's so easy to launch right into a lesson and forget to notice a new haircut, new glasses, missing teeth, lower speaking voices, subtle use of make-up, or the blue ribbon won at a track meet. These interactions don't take long and can easily occur as students enter the room. They shouldn't distract from the lesson. Simple, authentic, human interactions build relationships and that's ultimately what leads to quality experiences for the teacher and learners.

Play it Forward—Planning for the Year

While I firmly believe teachers need to practice flexibility when planning, it's very helpful to have a sense of what and when certain events occur. Each August, I print a blank trimester template. It includes each grade, as well as trimester sections. This has become a ritual, much like filling in the blank plan book. It's proven to be a check system, as well as a guide, as I plan weekly/bi-weekly lessons. (A sample of this trimester guide is found on pages 69–71. It combines several parts of documents from the last few years.)

Other Considerations

When one considers how to design and implement curriculum, you recognize that teaching music is a sizeable job! Any level of instruction is designed with a magnitude of variables in mind—instructional time with students, resources and materials available, strengths of the teacher, etc.

The effective educator develops lessons to stimulate *all* of his or her students in ways that help them progress from simple understanding to appropriate application, regardless of minutes. A curriculum guide may provide the map, but it's the teacher who knows the destination and mode of travel.

With the vast array of choices (methods, systems, stages, frameworks) new music teachers might want to consider the following:

Remember why you like music

Musicians draw personal satisfaction and gratification while engaged in making music, either alone or with others. Provide opportunities for students to be engaged in the music-making process so that they too may reach a significant level of satisfaction. All effective educators agree that students deserve opportunities for meaningful and memorable experiences.

Draw on your strengths as a person, musician, educator

What is a strength? Something one does consistently well. Allow students to witness these strengths. One of the best lessons I observed involved a brand new teacher playing her cello to teach a multi-concept lesson; the fourth graders in the class were thoroughly enchanted, and they remembered the main points of the lesson!

Establish your priorities

Priorities are personal reflections of what an educator truly believes as important and valuable for his or her students. Keep them simple, keep them limited, and allow them to guide instructional design.

Seek the strength of your professional affiliations

There are many organizations to consider. I recommend membership in MENC: The National Association of Music Education, as it draws together music educators from every vein of instruction (preschool through doctoral programs). The MENC website (www.menc.org) is an excellent resource for curriculum design, lesson structure, unit planning, and other instructional ideas.

Know what the daily schedule looks like and how much time with students is available

There is an enormous difference between seeing students once a week or twice a week. There's also a substantial difference between 30-minute classes and 45-minute classes. Instructional time impacts what can be accomplished year to year. Music educators should advocate for acceptable and equitable time with students.

The best teachers teach children in a way that moves learning forward

Sometimes that forward action is barely perceived, making it easy to get frustrated. Keep the faith and keep the focus on what the students show and tell. Students have ways of letting a teacher know when they do not understand. That's when effective educators step back and follow a different path toward the same goals.

Remember that music class is instruction-based: it is, first and foremost, a place where learning occurs

Keeping that in mind, Eph Ehly reminds us that, "...a good teacher does not force-feed information. A good teacher encourages thinking. Therefore, even though you can't teach one to be musical, you can teach one to think musically. Effective teachers don't attempt to show their prowess, they encourage others to develop their own."[6]

Remember and recognize that learning is a process that occurs over time and is not limited to concepts and skills

Find routes that best help students' progress. Teaching cognitive skills and concepts is only part of the equation. Effective educators have a moral obligation to help the children in their classrooms find confidence and success as citizens of the world. Witnessing a young person's emergence as a fine human being is just about the best reward there is.

---

[6] Ehly, 37.

Sample Trimester Guide

Grade	First Trimester—*Sept/Oct/Nov*	Second Trimester—*Nov/Dec/Jan/Feb/Mar*	Third Trimester—*Mar/Apr/May/Jun*
K	Classroom procedures Space and movement Group vs. independent response/participation Song games Song stories	Steady beat vs. changing beat Singing voice vs. other voices Holiday sounds and songs Changes in music—showing enactively Patterns of long and short	Rhythmic icons—long, short, silence Patterns for improvising story with instruments Pitch—up/down/same Rhythm instruments—basic use and sound Summer styles (marching band, concert band, etc.)
1/ CLC	Classroom procedures Singing vs. other voices Steady beat Song games Using instruments for stories and songs Movement concepts Iconic rhythmic understanding	Expressive components—using vocabulary (louder than/softer than; faster than/slower than) Song stories/Compositions that tell stories Holiday songs and traditions Rhythm—Intro to symbolic notation Assess ability to keep steady beat	Instruments of the music room and in bands/orchestras Rhythmic notation—symbolic system Simple form—sight/sound/motion Parent sharing
2/ CLC	Classroom procedures Singing voice standard Song games Singing independently Reading, writing, playing basic rhythms Basic form—verse/phrase/repetition	Rhythmic independence—in games, notation, dictation Holiday singing and culture reference Songs and events of the holidays (*The Nutcracker* unit) Pitch—same/different/upward/downward Poetry and lyrics in melodic setting	Instrument classification, particularly percussion Meter and time signature—bottom-number meaning Location of notes on staff—"on the line," "in the space" Parent sharing

Grade	First Trimester—Sept/Oct/Nov	Second Trimester—Nov/Dec/Jan/Feb/Mar	Third Trimester—Mar/Apr/May/Jun
3/ CLC	Classroom procedures Unison singing; singing two-part rounds Following melody/rhythm Meter/time signature Reading, writing, playing extended rhythms Listening and interpreting Accompanying songs with instruments	Tchaikovsky and *The Nutcracker* Style lessons involving "'Twas the Night Before Christmas" Famous holiday pieces Accompanying songs using instruments Rhythmic independence—notation; staying on part while counterpoint occurs	Metric recognition through listening Understanding and application of top time-signature number Instrument classification—woodwind/brass Accompaniments to songs—three independent parts Art Gala performance
4/ CLC	Unison and round singing Instrument families—identification (sight/sound) Rhythm writing, reading, playing Reading, interpreting, creating score Performance practice with singing	Holiday songs and traditions Form composition project Prominent composers and their influence Continued unison and rounds; partner songs Mixed meter; recognition of meter within compositions	Revisit wind/strings/percussion instruments Songs of the Pacific Northwest Marimba ensembles Performance—in classes or with others
5/ CLC	Unison and round singing Rhythmic/melodic/score interpretation Patriotic songs—background, memory Drumming ensemble project	Part-singing—role of melody vs. harmony Voicings—soprano/alto/tenor/bass Melodic composition project Holiday compositions (*Messiah* study) Holiday songs, especially arrangements for marimba	Level I, Guitar unit—folk songs with simple chords American Music Project—composers; styles Performance—Musical theatre

Grade	First Trimester — *Sept/Oct/Nov*	Second Trimester — *Nov/Dec/Jan/Feb/Mar*	Third Trimester — *Mar/Apr/May/Jun*
6/ CLC	Unison and round singing Singing of African, Cuban and Caribbean songs Rhythmic/melodic/score interpretation Patriotic songs—background, memory Advanced drumming techniques Adenkum songs	Level II, Guitar unit—composing for guitar; advanced progression; listening and styles log Holiday songs, accompanied by guitar and marimba arrangements	Marimba ensembles—Jazz, Caribbean, African Culminating composition project Sixth-grade variety show—organization, planning and performances
Ensembles	Chorus (start week 3) Songs to include *a cappella* singing, Hebrew texts, Latin texts, sacred/secular Preparation for December programs Observation of SVJH chorus	Holiday performances Discussion and planning for sixth-grade marimba ensemble (begins early March)	Sixth-grade marimba ensemble rehearsals and performances

Bringing Heart Inside the Music Classroom
(Without Getting Hammered)

Everyone I've ever met has an innate desire to be liked and to be appreciated. Some show that need in more obvious ways than others, but it's there. Mutual kindness—one human to another—feels 'right'. In the classroom, however, there are times when a teacher doesn't feel liked or appreciated. Conditions can exist where the mind and spirit simply want to cry out "Why are you kids treating me this way? What did I ever do to you?"

Expecting all students to accept kindness graciously or to generate kindness is not part of the reality of teaching in the twenty-first century. While I believe being kind is an innate human condition, there are children who arrive at school with that part of their biological framework dormant, squelched, ignored, or damaged.

While it is a dismal and frustrating reality, some students in our schools lack the basic needs of compassion, attention and love. Some have been neglected or largely ignored during their infancy and pre-operational years. According to Lazear, "The neglected infant syndrome results in attachment issues. The early interaction between parent and child profoundly affects a child's ability to learn, adapt, and socially interact."[1]

Caine and Caine wrote:

> The first 5 years of life are the most critical to the development of a psychologically healthy adult. The environment affects the brain physiologically. If, beginning tomorrow, we did nothing more than protect children

---

[1] Edward P. Lazear, editor, *Education in the Twenty-first Century* (Stanford, CA: Hoover Institute Press Publications, Stanford University, 2002) 155.

72

from destructive experiences closely linked to some form of abandonment, we would have an emotionally healthier, brighter generation twenty years from now.[2]

If that's the case, what can we do about those first five years? Mourn when children show evidence of lost opportunities and thank the parents of those children arriving squared away, ready to learn. Do know that both of these groups will be in our classrooms. One quickly discovers that children come to school with a varied capacity to learn. Truthfully, some students in our schools are simply trying to survive.

Regardless of school readiness or emotional state, all children deserve teachers who will care about them and will value them as respected human beings of unlimited potential. In most cases, we can't change what a home life is like, but we can and should establish a school environment that reflects a decent, respectful image of how an adult can behave. It is not easy, but I do believe it's possible for students to learn and practice habits of courtesy, kindness, empathy, and citizenship.

Given that today's children come to school with a mixture of emotional, psychological and cognitive skills and abilities, how do we organize our classrooms in such a way that all students feel safe, welcomed, liked, and appreciated for who they are? How can we protect our own emotions from coiling with frustration when a child refuses to follow directions or when he or she turns the classroom into an arena of outbursts, physical aggression, quiet bullying, and threats? How can we establish a classroom where learning happens, the individual is celebrated (and protected), and a sense of community is created?

In this chapter, generalizations as well as details of classroom management are shared. Much of the narrative is derived from real classroom situations I've experienced. In my opinion, this chapter embraces the most vital information for all educators to consider as they go inside the music classroom.

Tough Skin, Kind Heart

What's one of the things each new teacher is told? Develop tough skin. Admittedly, I was a bit naive as to the potential volatility of human nature early in my career. My childhood was fairly ideal: I had a family that loved me, was popular with friends and teachers, and earned accolades from various universities. I was well liked, appreciated, respected, and en-

---

[2] Caine and Caine, 32–33.

couraged every step of the way. My experience with people (children or adults) who were mean, unkind or psychologically unstable was limited.

Since that first year, I've learned to not be shocked by the range of student apathy, anger or distrust apparent in many schools. I'm saddened by its existence, but no longer surprised by the explosiveness of some children. "Show respect to you? Why? Who are you, anyway? Just another adult telling me what to do and when to do it! Get out of my face!" (shouted by a third grader my second year of teaching).

How did I react? I wanted to cry! I wanted to snarl my face to show him how much bigger and tougher I was. The truth? My feelings were deeply hurt by an eight year old. It was the first of many interactions I would have with angry children. What has changed over the years? My skin has toughened and I've learned to control my reactions—well, most of the time.

The stories of children's lives and what many endure are heartbreaking as well as inconceivable when compared to the life everyone deserves. The big 'however' is that we have the opportunity to give *all* students a glimpse of what a consistent and caring adult looks like, sounds like and feels like.

When the heart is considered in our daily interactions with children, we hold the potential to save lives. Although it may sound cliché, I believe it to be true. It doesn't mean we let children rule the classroom, either. We all know kids want and need structure. I believe our students desire and deserve adults who will be the adult in the classroom—an adult who will advocate for a learning environment that functions for everyone, and care enough for the students to consistently make it so.

Pagel and Spevacek wrote:

We have no control over our students' home environments (prior to school habits). We do have control over what goes on inside the classroom once students arrive. It's up to teachers to prepare themselves, set the stage, and accept responsibility of each student's educational outcome. (Teachers should) dedicate themselves to teaching their students until they learn.[3]

Learning can't occur inside a classroom that is unsafe or unstable. Children, and adults, for that matter, cannot fully function in chaos. Effective educators establish a climate where the heart of teaching is evident but protected from getting

---

[3] Pagel and Spevacek, 7.

'hammered'. In order for this to occur, we must develop techniques and skills that allow students to learn and us to teach in an environment that is safe and promotes human dignity.

The 'Looks Like, Sounds Like, Feels Like' System

Classroom management is a must for *every teacher* at *every grade level* in *every situation*. It is not simple, but it is essential. Over the years, I've developed a system of classroom management that has served me fairly well. For lack of a better title, I refer to it as the 'Looks like, Sounds like, Feels like' method. It is characterized by a set of instructional statements that describe what students will look like when they do a certain activity, what it will sound like when they execute this activity, and what it will feel like while they're doing it. For example:

> Third-grade students enter the music room. The teacher welcomes them, with instructions to find a space in the room. The teacher describes what he sees, hears and feels: "I see people walking to a space. Their arms are down and their feet stay on the floor. I hear people using inside voices and asking others to please move and give them their space back. I get the feeling you are ready to hear the next instruction, since your eyes are on me and your mouths are closed."

All of this is communicated in less than one or two minutes. If understood clearly, I see 26 eight-year-old children standing in their own spaces with their minds focused on the activity, safe and ready to hear the next bit of information.

In my music classes, these interactions are repeated for each and every activity. Yes, it's exhausting; however, students begin to intrinsically know what to do. If their actions indicate misunderstanding or confusion, or they aren't intrinsically adhering to what's expected, then every step is repeated. They leave the room and we start again. It's not punitive—it is merely an expectation that requires more practice.

How many times will the students need to practice an activity before it becomes habit? *As many times as it takes!* I had a class of first graders who needed those clear 'Looks like, Sounds like, Feels like' instructions pretty much all year long. I remember on the 105th day of school, we were still working on entering the room. Their classroom teacher agreed that repeating the expectation with practice was necessary to keep this particular blend of personalities safe.

Communicating what is expected is crucial; meaning it is more critical. This sounds so simple since it's easy to 'just assume' kids know what is wanted. Effective teachers know that's not the case. Every activity in the music room comes with a set of expectations that are grade- and age-level appropriate. These must be understood by all learners.

When expectations are articulated clearly and backed up with practice and consistency, the classroom functions in a manner conducive to learning. That's my goal with the 'Looks like, Sounds like, Feels like' method.

This system includes the following six steps and is based on direct communication, modeling and practice. (A graphic representation of these steps is found on the facing page.)

1. The teacher describes what he or she wants the activity to look like, sound like and feel like.
2. The teacher models what it will look like, sound like and feel like.
3. The students practice.
4. The strategy or movement or activity is executed.
5. Everyone involved considers how well it worked.
6. Students begin to intrinsically execute various activities without the narrative voice of the teacher.

About the 'Looks Like, Sounds Like, Feels Like' Method of Classroom Management

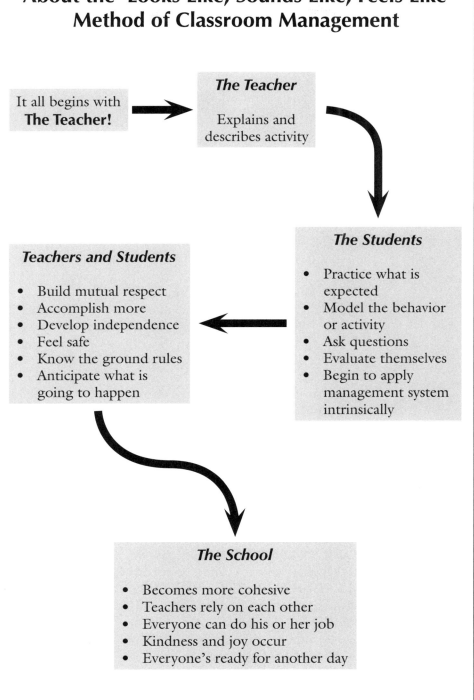

It all begins with **The Teacher!**

The Teacher

Explains and describes activity

The Students

- Practice what is expected
- Model the behavior or activity
- Ask questions
- Evaluate themselves
- Begin to apply management system intrinsically

Teachers and Students

- Build mutual respect
- Accomplish more
- Develop independence
- Feel safe
- Know the ground rules
- Anticipate what is going to happen

The School

- Becomes more cohesive
- Teachers rely on each other
- Everyone can do his or her job
- Kindness and joy occur
- Everyone's ready for another day

At any given time, the teacher returns to step one and proceeds through the motions again. Does it get old? Yes. Does it prevent most disruptions in the classroom? *Yes!* Being able to teach without constant disruptions is ideal. I tell my students that I love to teach, but I don't like to be in charge of their behavior all the time. It makes me grumpy. This seems to motivate them to keep disruptions to a minimum. They also are eager to get on with our activities and avoid repeating instructions if at all possible.

What's the rule?

Even with the best of teachers, occasional derailing occurs. A student walks in from the playground with some frustrating situation; a new boy arrives in fifth or sixth grade and is anxious to prove his status as the new 'alpha male'; or a child throws up, right on the drum. It happens! In fact, each of these scenarios occurred in my room. I believe they all occurred during the same week. Experience teaches flexibility and to be ready for just about anything.

In his book, *Teacher Man,* Frank McCourt described his early years of teaching and mentions the stories he would share with his students in an effort to entertain as well as teach. In this chapter, I've included a few of my own stories that point out particular management situations. In all cases, the stories are true but the names have been changed to protect the innocent (just like in the old TV show, *Dragnet*). Each story ends with a rule to consider and reflect on. Some of the stories are a bit comical now that I look back on them; some still make me want to cry.

Sixth Graders Who Sabotage

Habits are powerful. My first year at my present school demonstrated this fact in profound ways. The sixth graders had developed habits in music class the years prior to my arrival that they were unwilling and reluctant to alter.

I'd not really considered how habits could control one's motivation or attitude until I started teaching these sixth graders new songs. Their reaction to my form of teaching quickly indicated how it differed from their previous music teacher. They weren't ready to 'play the game' my way.

In the first five minutes several things became quickly evident: 1. They did not find any need to sing with any quality whatsoever; 2. They did not see how learning about music

So, Now What?

When I was pregnant with our first child, I read every book I could about the first months of life, giving birth, taking care of your infant, etc. I was well informed intellectually, physically and (I thought) emotionally. No amount of reading could prepare my husband and me for the real thing! With experience, however, our second child was much less confounding and confusing. This is sort of like understanding the full management picture via reading about it and college classroom discussions only.

While it's next to impossible to duplicate the authentic experience of classroom management in a contrived setting, here are some recommendations that might help prepare you for the real thing:

Before entering the classroom as a certified teacher:

- Be with students—volunteer!
- Observe teachers who have a reputation for being good managers.
- Consider how you handle disruptions in your personal life.
- Learn to take advice, apologize, move on, and forgive.
- Watch children in public places; observe the variety of behaviors you'll see.

When interviewing for a teaching position, seek opportunities to learn as much as you can about the school's climate and attitude toward behavior:

- Does the school have a published classroom-management policy?
- When the students are in music class, what options exist, and what kind of support will exist from classroom teachers and/or administrators?
- Be aware of the culture of the school.
- Ask how students perceived going to music class with the previous music teacher.
- Is there a mentor program in the district, or in the school?
- Look at the music room and envision how to make it the most inviting and welcoming environment possible.

Before the students arrive:

- Ask other teachers about their discipline plans. View the models of experienced educators.
- Establish traffic patterns for students: where should they enter and where should they exit?
- Borrow the money (if necessary) to buy a 'grown-up' repertoire of clothes to wear. Be comfortable, but establish the look of 'I'm the adult here'.
- Plan to spend time in the classroom; get a feel for it. Make the facility function in way that helps you and students.

Finally, when the students arrive:

- Meet them at the door. Greet and welcome them.
- Before they enter, tell them what you want to see and hear as they come into the room.
- Have materials ready for use. Lag time can destroy the flow of any lesson, good or bad.
- Positive statements should be said often, nothing 'mushy' or half true. Describe what the students are doing that fits the plan. "Yep, looks like you heard what I said and you're following those instructions like pros! This looks like a great class!"
- Be flexible, be organized, be accommodating, and be the adult.

One final bit of advice and caution—if the management system established is not working, a teacher should first look to him or herself. If, however, the setting and situation is dangerous or at an impasse, seek the assistance of colleagues, mentors and administrators. Educators have the right to expect some level of support from their school, particularly as a new employee.

Each and every educator *deserves* opportunities for success. Spend the first year as a teacher surrounded by people who will lend support, advice and an ear of wisdom. *Succeed.* Everyone has challenging children now and then, but no one deserves to teach in a place with equally challenging adults (see Chapter 6 for more details). Success is far more possible with a supportive faction of adults offering assistance and guidance.

New teachers experience substantial trials in the day-to-day business of teaching. Any degree of uncertainty can be regarded as momentary mountains to cross. One should not, however, experience continuous feelings of abandonment and solitude when it comes to solving classroom management issues. Ask others for help! If you've found the 'right' place to begin your career, assistance is only one room away.

One final word on classroom management—Hiam Ginnot reminds us:

> I've come to the frightening conclusion that I am the decisive element in the classroom. It's my personal approach that creates the climate. It's my daily mood that makes the weather. As a teacher, I possess a tremendous power to make a child's life miserable or joyous. I can be a tool of torture or an instrument of inspiration. I can humiliate or humor, hurt or heal. In all situations, it is my response that decides whether a crisis will be escalated or deescalated and a child humanized or dehumanized.[4]

Be the adult your students will trust. Find the best way for them to learn. Rely on other adults in the building. Persevere. Look for paths over the mountains so that magic can be experienced. Keep bringing the heart into the classroom—and remember that no one deserves to have it hammered away.

---

[4] Randy Sprick, et al. *The Safe and Civil Schools Series: Proactive, Positive, and Instructional Discipline* CD-ROM (Eugene, OR: Safe and Civil Schools, 2005).

Above and Beyond the Music Classroom

Most elementary general music teachers have exceptionally full days, meeting and greeting class after class, one right after the other. I've taught as many as ten 35-minute classes a day (due to an extended schedule in our school) to a comfortably paced six classes a day (45-minute sections with a *real* lunch and planning period; luxury!). Given the 'busy-ness' of the day-in-day-out schedule, why entertain any discussion regarding 'above and beyond' the basic responsibilities of the elementary general music teacher?

Throughout my career I have yet to meet a general music teacher whose position does not include one or more of the following 'above and beyond' activities:

- Maintains an ensemble during lunch, planning period, or outside of the school day (before or after school).
- Plans and prepares students for performances at assemblies. (In most cases, the music teacher is usually responsible for many of these assemblies, music performances included or not.)
- Arranges for and promotes evening programs involving students, parents, teachers, and community.
- Organizes special events and/or field trips for students to hear or see a significant musical event occurring outside of the school.

In most situations going above and beyond the teaching of six or seven or ten classes is just 'part of the gig'. (Hopefully, most districts across the country compensate the music teacher's time beyond the contracted day. This is the first position I've held that includes funds for additional responsibilities.)

Experiences for students that extend beyond the general music classes are sometimes included in a job description. Sometimes they begin as a result of the music teacher's desire to work with a select group of students, while in other circumstances, they represent what the community has come to expect. Regardless of their origins or reason for existing, above and beyond musical experiences (ensembles, parent programs, assembly performances) should be perceived as positives, since they provide an excellent means of increasing the learning and commitment level of students.

This chapter includes details for organizing and/or maintaining performance-based ensembles, with particular attention to choral groups. In addition, suggestions and ideas for putting together music programs for predetermined grade levels are included. This advice is offered from my own experience; there are many models for new educators to consider as each school setting offers its own degree of variability.

At the end of the chapter, selected letters, announcements, performance criteria, etc. are included. The reader is welcome to use them as templates.

Ensemble Experiences

Over the past several years, in multiple settings, I've heard and seen elementary general music teachers providing a variety of ensemble possibilities, including:

- Chorus
- Drama/Music Theater
- Recorder Consort
- Marimba Ensembles
- "Orff-estras" (Orff instrument ensembles)
- Drumming Club
- Folk Dance Groups
- Percussion Ensemble
- Guitar Ensemble

Participation in these groups was either 'ya'll come'-based (whoever shows up is welcome), by invitation only, or auditioned, with limited grade level involvement.

The General Music Teacher as Ensemble Director

In my career as a music educator, I've initiated or inherited a choral ensemble each and every year taught. It's taken on many shapes, sizes, age groups, and settings. Currently, I maintain a choral ensemble of fifth and sixth graders through my school.

My early experience with choirs was limited to third through fifth graders at my first school. Eventually, I moved from one state to another and accepted a position as co-director of a highly select (and visible) auditioned choir, ages 10–14. Like everything else in my teaching career, both ensemble experiences were new and slightly intimidating. I was fortunate to be surrounded by colleagues who served as mentors and helped me move from basic 'arm waving' to functioning more effectively as conductor.

Initially trained as a band director, I found choirs to be exciting, unique and aligned with my interests in improved singing instruction. I discovered that directing a chorus calls for musical *and* social savvy, as well instructional know-how.

I was curious to find out how the best children's choir directors organize and teach their ensemble members, so I decided to evolve that curiosity into a doctoral dissertation. I'm eternally grateful to my graduate committee for allowing such a practical topic to be accepted!

The common characteristics I observed in extraordinarily gifted children's choir directors included their ability to:

- Establish who could, would and should participate in their groups.
- Teach toward musicianship and musical understanding.
- Select repertoire that would not only 'fit' the group, but would be representative of superb quality for children's voices.
- Instruct children to sing well, developing habits necessary for healthy and beautiful tones.
- Maintain a positive culture of learning, contributing, and artistic growth.[1]

---

[1] Patricia Bourne, "Instructional Techniques of Outstanding Children's Choir Directors" (Ed. D. diss., Arizona State University, Tempe, 1990.)

These characteristics are definitely what I strive to incorporate as the director of our school's choir. All effective music educators establish their own norms when organizing an ensemble like a chorus. Mine are based on what I learned through observation, what I've learned how to do, who I have as students, what my school community will support, and what seems to work year after year.

Establishing and Teaching the Elementary Chorus

That being said, here's what I've learned and practiced over my 26 years of conducting school, church, community, district, regional, honors, and all-state choirs. These parameters and tips are not necessarily restricted to choral ensembles; they can be applied to any kind of ensemble, at any level.

1. Establish rules for membership in the ensemble.

If one decides to make it a ya'll come group, that's fine. However, be aware that a ya'll come group can quickly turn into 'ya'll come...and ya'll go'. It may become difficult to maintain any semblance of forward progress with this kind of system. Students in my fifth/sixth-grade chorus are invited to membership, based on three criteria:

- Their disposition for singing as witnessed in the general music class. (Do they participate? Do they employ techniques we've talked about in class regarding best singing? Do they listen effectively while others sing? Do they have reasonably open minds to singing in multiple languages and styles?)
- Their attitude toward following my instructional advice. (If I suggest they raise their eyebrows slightly, what do I see them doing? If I suggest they place their hands loosely at their sides, what happens? If I suggest a re-shaping of the mouth in order to produce a clearer tone, do they giggle only, or maybe giggle, then do it?)
- Their ability to utilize self-control and self-management, behaviorally. (Do they exhibit enough control of their arms, feet, hands, and mouth to allow me to teach and others to learn? Do they help the instructional climate of the room?)

Note that singing 'in tune' is not one of my criteria. I believe 99% of students, even those unsure singers, will improve vocally throughout the year as a result of the specific vocal instruction offered through choral participation. To me, attitude is everything. I have faith in my ability to teach in-tune singing as part of their overall musical skills *if* they are inclined to accept my instructional advice.

Accompanying the letter of invitation is a one-page contract. The contract asks for three signatures: the student, the student's parent and the student's classroom teacher. All three are vital. The student promises to contribute to the group, to come ready for rehearsal (the contract describes in detail what that means), to participate in the performances, and to be a positive influence on the entire ensemble. The parent promises to properly attire their choir member, transport their child to evening events, and encourage continued membership throughout the year (even when baseball season starts). The classroom teacher offers support by allowing the student to participate in performances (particularly those that occur during the school day) and helps circulate communiqués from me to the student.

I bring these contracts to rehearsals throughout the fall. When I see a student showing behaviors contradictory to what they promised, I dig out that contract and strongly suggest they remember and respect what they agreed to do.

Membership in the group is contingent on returning the contract in a timely manner with all the necessary signatures. It's also necessary that they attend each rehearsal with the appropriate spirit engaged.

2. Establish the rehearsal time frame and setting.

When I interviewed for my current school, the chorus met right in the middle of the morning, prime classroom time for the teachers. Many of the fifth and sixth teachers wanted to see chorus dropped. I wanted it to stay. We needed to compromise. Our staff resolved to keep the group but moved rehearsals to the last hour of the school day. The rehearsal schedule has changed twice since then but has settled into the present time frame: after school, once a week for one hour.

The membership has been consistently large, necessitating a space bigger than the music room. Each Wednesday when the closing bell rings, I employ the muscle of various chorus members to roll the piano into the gym. I hurriedly get the environment ready for chorus, transforming it from a physical education classroom to a choral rehearsal room. Within 5 to 10 minutes, chorus members are on the steps leading to the stage, ready for warm-ups. I have everything I need ready to transport from the music room so that rehearsal can begin quickly. Every minute counts when you meet only once a week.

3. Determine what kind of support personnel and resources you need to help students excel in the ensemble.

I'm a real 'boom-chick' pianist. When I play the piano, I cannot teach effectively; I think about my fingers and the missed notes rather than listen to the singers. In order to perform the level of music I enjoy hearing my children sing, a bona-fide accompanist is required. I've been exceptionally fortunate to find just the right person at the right time. In most years, my accompanist was a parent; in others, it was a colleague from another school in our district. Most recently, a high school senior aligned her accompanying experience to fit her senior project. In all cases, our chorus has sung with greater proficiency with someone (*anyone*) other than me behind the keyboard!

As far as resources go, I use a sound system (for amplification of my voice and soloists), a CD player (to occasionally listen to other choirs on recording), and, of course, the piano for live accompaniment. Our rehearsals are often videotaped: That equipment is included in the pile of materials to set up and get ready each week.

4. Select repertoire that 'fits' the group, the audience and the director's skills, and stretches the musicianship of everyone involved.

They say variety is the spice of life and that's certainly true when it comes to selecting music. I find something appealing in all kinds of choral styles and, fortunately, there are prolific composers who have focused on providing quality literature for children's voices. Seeking the 'right' music is an essential activity for the director. How does one find pieces to choose from?

Each summer I attend some kind of choral reading session or workshop. These can be found all over the country and are excellent venues for singing and evaluating new literature. Referrals from other children's choir directors work beautifully, as well. I try to attend concerts featuring children's choirs and listen to available CDs for repertoire options. There are numerous retailers, publishers and professional organizations that sponsor summer reading sessions. These workshops can be found in all geographical regions and are affordable, informative and fun to attend. These events are always advertised on publisher's and music vendor's Web sites.

When faced with a stack of music to peruse, some kind of system is needed for narrowing the range of choices. The master teachers I observed provided an excellent criteria list for identifying repertoire for their choirs. I've incorporated their tips into my process:

- Consideration of the text (What words are sung? How are they set? Are they age-appropriate?)
- If the words are original (not based on existing poetry), do they have merit? Can they stand on their own, artistically?
- Harmonic variety (Hearing all major-key pieces sung in unison is certainly not as interesting as mixed voicing and tonality.)
- Range and tessitura (Does it fit the age and particular group I'm directing? Is it appropriate for the size of my ensemble?)

- The accompaniment (How does it relate to and enhance the piece as a whole? Is some enhancement suggested, such as drums, a flute obbligato, a bass part,
  etc.?)
- The inherent value of the work (It does not have to be
  'high brow' to be considered artistic, but will the piece
  showcase my group's strengths?)
- The pedagogical merits (What can I teach through the
  piece?)
- Level of challenge for my students (I don't want my
  singers to be stagnant. Introducing a piece that stretch-
  es them is appealing to us all, but I do want to be sure
  adequate rehearsal time is available to reach success
  and satisfaction with more challenging repertoire.)
- Stylistic characteristics (Does the music fit specific stylistic qualities?)
- The inherent beauty and appeal for the singers, director and audience (We often overlook ourselves, but it's
  really difficult to teach a piece I don't like or in which
  I find little value.)

Selecting the music they sing is a timely process *and* a costly
one. It's critical to exercise some kind of criteria system when
faced with heaping mounds of octavos and song collections.

5. Communicate, in writing, with the critical members of the ensemble.

Critical members include (in most cases) students, parents, teachers, and administrators. People's lives are incredibly complicated these days: there are *so* many things added to the typical family schedule. Parents must be given time to adjust their calendars to include all details associated with membership (delivery and pick-up times, concert dates and locations, attire, etc.). Since our classroom teachers are involved (adding their approval for membership), they deserve to be included in the communication loop.

The better the communication, the more thorough the support. In reality, I'm a bit of an overachiever in this category; however, I rarely have a confused student or parent. We consistently experience 100% attendance at performances, which makes communicating so thoroughly well worth it. (See pages 112 and 113 for examples of my communiqués.)

6. Decide when and where performances will be held and follow protocol to 'book it'.

Parents make a superb audience. Personally, I burst with pride and excitement when I watch my own children perform on stage or on the risers—my eyes can't get enough of watching my own progeny in the spotlight! The opportunity for students to show their moms and dads what they've learned and are able to do can't be replicated. However, I've found providing diverse audiences for my ensembles to be exceptionally valuable, as well.

Finding venues away from school takes time and knowledge. One must figure out who to call, where to look, what procedures and assumptions to operate with, etc. The following is a typical checklist I follow when scheduling mid-December off-campus performances.

- **Late August:** Contact venues. If there's a Web site that allows for online registering, that's great; however, I've found talking to a representative of the venue to be more secure.
- **Early September:** Reserve the date and time for my school-based performances (the dates go to our school secretary and webmaster, for publication).
- **Mid-September:** Obtain necessary paperwork in order to get permission from my administrator for off-campus performances.

- **Early October:** Publicize all performance dates—places and times included—to parents, teachers, students, office manager, webmaster, administrator, etc.
- **Early November:** Circulate volunteer list to solicit chaperones and other adult helpers required for off-campus performances.
- **Late November:** If I've never seen the venue, I go there to 'walk the walk' my students will follow. Timing is crucial when a performance is involved, and I want to understand how long it takes to get from the entrance of a building to the green room to the stage and out again
- **Early December:** Distribute field trip permission slips and select a return date.
- **Week of the off-campus performance:** Send one last written communiqué to parents, especially chaperones, and an email reminder to our entire staff, particularly the food-service staff (since 80–100 students will not be there for lunch).

I believe special groups deserve special places to perform. I do everything I can to help make that possible. If the students are relatively mature, responsible and musical, they deserve to be heard by an expanded audience base.

7. Ensure that ensemble members look like they belong to each other.

Concert or performance attire is part of being in a special ensemble. Whether students wear matching T-shirts or simple black and white, looking similar to each other elevates the feeling of community and responsibility of one ensemble member to the next. In my first year of teaching, my principal asked about performance attire for our chorus. She was one of the first to indicate how vital it was that the kids were connected visually. She assured me this would elevate their level of performance and behavior, as well. She was right. We found a parent who could negotiate a reasonable price for T-shirts and printed them with our school colors. My first chorus looked sharp in purple and white. They looked like a choral ensemble and behaved admirably.

Our fifth/sixth-grade chorus members wear black on the bottom and white on the top. The boys add a turquoise-colored tie while the girls have the same color in a ribbon that loops around the collar of a blouse. They look like they belong together and respond in positive ways to appearing dressed up. For many of the guys, it is their first experience with a tie. The difference a dress shirt and tie makes in their 'gentlemanly behavior' is astounding. And, of course, it's a huge boost to their egos when members of the staff comment on how handsome they look.

Equally vital is how I look. It's important to dress in a manner that complements what the kids are wearing, as well as one that doesn't distract from them. I don't want to block the visual image *they* project. In almost all cases, I wear black and keep jewelry to a minimum. The audiences we tend to perform for are there to see and hear the students, not to watch me.

8. Plan the ensemble rehearsal in such a way that rituals and routines are established.

Habits are formed through repetition. If I want to make the most of our rehearsal time, students must learn habits to function in a way that maximizes each minute of our time together. Routines are introduced day one. Chorus members learn my expectations of rehearsal protocol by seeing a visual of the typical schedule we maintain:

3:00–3:10	Go to bathroom, get drink, find place on the steps or risers
3:10–3:20	Warm-ups and vocal techniques

3:20–3:35	Song introduction or review #1
3:35–3:37	Stretch break (often, I use this time to make announcements)
3:37–3:55	Song introduction or review #2
3:55–4:00	Listening and evaluating performance (I videotape our rehearsals, so we'll often watch a snippet of the previous rehearsal. Or we listen to a recording that models a technique we're working on)
4:00–4:15	Song introduction or review #3
4:15–4:20	Last-minute announcements
4:20	Dismissal

During the first rehearsal, I'll present a list of what I expect of chorus members and what they can and should expect from me. Every year, I repeat this process, even with returning members. It's usually very quiet in the room when this list is revealed, which tells me they respect the mutual honor we both bring to the group. I also think the words included in this list have deep meaning—"dignity," "pride," "artists/musicians," "ambassadors"—this kind of language reflects the vision I have for the group. The fifth- and sixth-grade members are old enough to 'get it' and respond appropriately.

When students know what is expected of them and what they can expect from me there are very few surprises. It places responsibility on all of us.

The fifth/sixth-grade chorus at my current school existed prior to my tenure. It required adjustments but was primarily a continuation of a preexisting group. Beginning a brand new ensemble requires similar tactics to those described in this chapter. This was certainly the case when I decided to offer an additional ensemble experience at my school.

The Sixth-Grade Marimba Ensemble

The Parent Teacher Association at my school has graciously provided financial assistance for purchasing a variety of instruments. Since my arrival in 1995, we have added an abundance of drums, guitars, small classroom instruments, and Orff instruments. Of all the things to play in our room, none is more popular than the marimbas.

I'm fortunate to have a variety of marimbas in my music classroom. These instruments have enhanced my students' musicianship in all respects: Their skills in composition, improvisation, theoretical understanding, music reading, tonal sense, and rhythmic accuracy have profited from having them available.

In addition to the instructional attributes of the instruments, I always enjoy hearing the marimbas played by my students. I've grown more secure in my ability to teach specific concepts through the use of the instruments. After five years of adding marimbas to my general music instruction, I sensed it was time to start a special ensemble in order to take those skills one step farther for the students and for me.

Two years ago, I began an after-school marimba group available to sixth graders only and operating for part of the year (March–June). By deciding to offer this ensemble, I used a similar 'recipe' that existed with the chorus:

1. Create a means to solicit and select members.
2. Establish when and where to rehearse.
3. Determine the kind of support and resources needed.
4. Research and select repertoire with criteria for that process.
5. Establish rules and lines of communication with everyone involved.
6. Set performance dates and venues.
7. Decide on performance attire.
8. Articulate and define what the rules, rituals and routines of rehearsal would look like and sound like.

The students who participated in *Chiviriku Ridza* (the name of our ensemble; meaning "active beat" in Shona, a prominent language of Zimbabwe) committed to practicing on their own and with others during recesses, attending rehearsals twice a week, setting up and tearing down instruments for rehearsal and performance settings, and helping members who struggled with particular sections of any given piece.[2] It was an honor and pleasure to watch the group function. Their greatest achievement was observed in the last performance when the group performed onstage with student-only leadership. I sat in the audience, thrilled for them and exceptionally proud of their musicianship and level of confidence.

At the end of both seasons, I asked ensemble members to share the best part of being in the group. Their answers blended with the philosophical reasons I believe ensembles belong (and often thrive) in the elementary school setting:

1. The level of musicianship is raised.
2. Students belong to something that has high achievement goals.
3. Friendships are made through mutual responsibility and commitment.
4. Hard work pays off and has its rewards.
5. The music calls for concentrated efforts and practice.
6. Maturity of thought and action is the expectation.
7. Mutual respect is a must, between ensemble members and director.
8. The audiences learn new musical styles and get a sense of the musical skills upper-elementary students are capable of possessing.

[2] Included on page 114 is the "Requirements for Participation in Marimba Ensemble" that I distribute to all interested students.

9. The director's musical sensitivity, knowledge and skill increase.
10. The school can boast that unique experiences exist for its students.

As mentioned earlier in the chapter, the above and beyond ensemble is created either from a teacher's desire to direct a special group or inherited from what's always existed at a particular school. I believe teaching one's classes is a full-time job; the addition of an established ensemble (that might not match an educator's skills or passions) is exceedingly difficult to maintain. Obviously, there is quite a bit of work involved with performance-based groups.

My advice? If an ensemble is expected to be a part of your teaching schedule, you should be allowed to exercise flexibility and propose a group that benefits from your strength and passions.

Throughout my tenure as an elementary general music teacher, I've seen experienced music educators willingly and eagerly share their time and knowledge with new teachers. If establishing and maintaining an ensemble is important to a new teacher, then he or she need not look very far to find help. The central ingredients for the general music teacher to establish a performing ensemble are organization, commitment to learn the craft, attitude, and passion.

Daytime and Evening Grade-Level-Based Performances

There are a few things one can count on as an elementary music teacher: he or she will teach all grade levels, encounter a wide diversity of skill and disposition for learning among his or her students, and will *definitely* have occasions when the entire community sees and hears the results of instruction. Performances for parents occur in each and every elementary school in the country, especially where a certified music educator teaches general music.

Personally, I look forward to the opportunity for my students to show what they know. The kids are thrilled to perform, particularly when they perceive their skills in a positive light. By the time my students reach the concert date, they've rehearsed each and every detail so that they can relax and enjoy the show. The best measurement of their success is the comments received after a concert: "I wish we could do it again!" "My family thought we were fantastic." "I thought I'd be nervous, but I wasn't." "Everyone was surprised at how great we sounded!" The students are proud, as they should be.

In order for an evening-type parent performance to flow smoothly, intricate steps must be considered and taught. Multiple variables go into any concert regardless of grade level, number of students involved, or musical skills demonstrated. The content of the program can represent everything from a themed concert to a published musical. Concerts can focus on demonstrating the multiple skills learned in music class (singing, dancing, instrument playing, reading notation, etc.). Regardless of content, the most important consideration is that students are set up for success.

Among the many pages of tips and advice I create for my student teachers is a timeline and checklist for preparing children for an evening performance event. I've relied on this list countless times as it reminds me of the details required for a successful event.

Countdown and Checklist for Evening Music Programs

Three to four months ahead of time (depending on how often one sees the students):

- ❏ Reserve the stage and any/all district equipment required (chairs, risers, tables, extended stage, platforms, etc.)
- ❏ Communicate ideas with the classroom teachers involved (this includes the physical education teacher(s) if the gym backs up to the stage)
  - ❏ Confirm the date of the performance with staff
  - ❏ Promote their assistance (help solicit parent help, if needed, include information in classroom newsletters, etc.)
- ❏ Inform office staff of the performance dates and which classes are involved
- ❏ Communicate with parents once the date is cleared through your staff
  - ❏ Inform them of the details—date, time, location, attire requirements (if any); how their child will be involved; etc. (See "A Day in Pike Street Market" on page 115 for an example.)

❑ Request assistance, if needed, with details of how help is needed (Sets? costumes? props?)
❑ Inform students (Describe the event in as many details as are appropriate for the grade level)
   ❑ Promote 'special jobs' (See "The 2006 Annual Sixth-Grade Varity Show—Ways to Be Involved" on page 116 for an example.)
   ❑ Begin describing and practicing what performance behavior will look like, sound like and feel like; this kind of instruction will continue throughout. (See "Performance Expectations" on page 117 for an example geared to first and second graders.)

One month ahead of concert:
❑ Solidify all musical numbers
❑ Circulate special-job sheet; ask students to pick their top three choices
   ❑ The jobs include tasks like speaking (introducing selections, etc.), distributing programs, moving equipment, playing an instrument, etc.
   ❑ All students should have a unique contribution—automatic buy-in and a reason to attend the evening performance
❑ Send reminder email to all staff impacted by group rehearsals, particularly those who are impacted by the time frame required for practice
❑ Prepare hand-out for program
   ❑ Include information that informs parents of the district or state Grade Level Expectations (GLEs) and/or standards attended to through the content of the program
   ❑ Be certain every child's name is included; ask for help in proofreading, particularly students' names

Two weeks prior to concert date:
❑ Begin rehearsing all music and activities in the order they will occur the night of the concert
❑ Make list of all props, instruments, sound equipment, and additional resources needed for group rehearsals
❑ Depending on grade level, ask students to make invitations for the staff, inviting them to the concert. Place them in teachers' mailboxes.
❑ Remind students of behavior expectations...constantly

One week before concert:
- ❑ Retrieve completed program from duplicating center
- ❑ If necessary, solicit the help of older, stronger children to help move heavy equipment (schedule during their recess breaks)
- ❑ Confirm behavior plan with classroom teachers and administrator (particularly if children with erratic behavior issues are involved in the concert)
- ❑ Circulate one last reminder to parents, in written form (See examples on pages 118 and 119.)
- ❑ Solidify with classroom teachers where students should go once they arrive for the concert (particularly essential for young students)
  - ❑ Options include music room, classroom, library, or (last resort) stage area
  - ❑ If a classroom teacher is unable to attend the evening concert, request a backup (particularly important for younger children)

Day of the concert:
- ❑ Set up the audience section, particularly if the stage is in the gym
  - ❑ If young children are assisting with chairs, double-check their spacing from one row to the next. (They tend to put one chair directly behind another, with little room for adult knees.)
  - ❑ Double-check custodial schedule, so that he or she knows when to unlock doors for admittance to the stage area
- ❑ Enjoy the event you and your students have worked toward

After the concert:
- ❑ Circulating some kind of thank-you note to classroom teachers, other helpful staff, and parent volunteers is usually appropriate and much appreciated
- ❑ Plan an appropriate celebration for the children involved in the program; include opportunities to discuss and evaluate overall performance. If the event was videotaped for educational purposes, this would be a perfect time to show it.

Other Performances

The extended list on the previous pages is suggested for those events that involve a large number of children in a time frame outside of their regular music class. General music teachers usually understand that a performance can be conceived in multiple ways: one student playing their recorder composition for another is a performance; one group singing a song they learned at camp is another; etc. An evening performance should be considered part of the process representative of a complete music education. The child's music instruction should include memorable events that go well beyond a single evening concert.

Should every grade level schedule a performance to occur after school hours for an extended audience? That's between the music educator and his or her classroom teachers and administrators. I know several elementary music teachers who schedule an evening performance for each and every grade. It's expected within their school culture. At my school, evening performances are not scheduled for each grade. My students demonstrate their skills through some kind of culminating event, but it isn't always scheduled to occur in an evening-concert format.

Performances are evident day to day. They are offered for other classrooms (scheduled ahead of time), for office staff

(spur of the moment), for classroom teachers (at the end of class), or for the custodian (who casually walks through now and then). At some point during the year, students do perform in a prescheduled event. Here's a sample of scheduled performance opportunities as they appeared during our 2004–2005 school year:

- **November:** Fourth graders performed as part of the Veteran's Assembly (daytime assembly)
- **December:** Fifth graders performed drumming ensembles and holiday pieces on recorder (scheduled during general music class time with invited guests attending)
- **March:** First and second graders performed short musical (evening)[3]
- **May:** Third graders performed during school's Art Gala (during the day)
- **June:** Sixth graders produced and performed in Variety Show (during the day)

Mixed among these dates were performances by fifth and sixth graders involved in chorus, band, strings, or marimba ensemble.

Why Go Above and Beyond?

Public performances, either through ensemble participation or grade level/classroom concerts, generate powerful learning opportunities for students. If strategically rehearsed, intricately involved and artistically challenged, students will not forget the experience and will be anxious for the next performance to occur. The emotional connection tied to these experiences will promote unique learning that isn't always possible in the day-in-day-out general music class.

Music is a social art. The music educator has an advantage over other teachers in the building in this area as there are unlimited chances to involve children in extraordinary experiences. When students are provided opportunities to go above and beyond in situations that involve their minds, bodies and hearts, they grasp the meaning and substance of music's unique contribution to other people's lives. Going above and beyond is well worth it.

---

[3] A more detailed timeline of this performance is offered on page 120.

To: Marimba Group Members and Parents

From: Mrs. Bourne
Date: April 17, 2006
Re: Updates

Calendar Updates, April 17–May 11

Please write down the following important dates:

Rehearsals:

Regular Monday/Friday, April 17, 21
Regular Monday/Friday, April 24, 28
No Rehearsal, Monday, May 1
Special rehearsal, Wednesday, May 3 (after school)
Regular Friday rehearsal, May 5
Regular Monday rehearsal, May 8
Special rehearsal, Tuesday, May 9 (lunch recess)
Special rehearsal, Wednesday, May 10

Field Trip:

Thursday, May 11th

Deadlines and Details

Permission slips for the May 11 field trip will be distributed on Friday, April 28. They are due one week later—May 5. **TURN YOUR COMPLETED PERMISSION SLIPS IN TO ME, NOT YOUR CLASSROOM TEACHER.** May 5th is also the day students must demonstrate their ability to play their parts in order to go on the field trip. Plan on maximum practice efforts in the next two weeks.

Special Guest on Friday!

On Friday (21st), Walt Hampton (composer of a bunch of our tunes!) will be here to work with you and give you tips on playing his compositions. Mr. Hampton is a music teacher in the tri-cities and a good friend. He is also one of the nation's leaders on African marimba music, having studied the music with master teachers from Zimbabwe. He will work you hard—I've asked him to! At the same time, you'll learn a great deal. Parents are welcome to attend this session (parents are also welcome to observe any of our rehearsals). We will end at the regular time of 4:20.

Chorus Checklist

Concert attire ready?

Students must wear concert attire to perform—no exceptions

Girls: Black knee-length (or longer) skirt or dress black slacks
Black shoes and black socks or black tights
White dress blouse (long-sleeve with a collar)

Boys: Black dress slacks
Black shoes and black socks
White dress shirt (long-sleeve with a strong collar)

Girls will be given fobs (ribbons) and boys will be given ties to wear.

Field trip permission forms in?

Friday, December 10 deadline
Remember to include $2.00 for the December 16th field trip

Concert dates on the calendar?

Tuesday, December 14: "Holiday Concert and Dessert"

Chorus members arrive by 6:30—Come to music room
Dessert and drink, $1.00—Concert itself is free
Skyview Junior High Choral groups, invited guests

Thursday, December 16: Performances at C.C. and Seattle

Chorus members wear concert attire to school
Get ties and fobs in music room, check in with teacher
Sing for Canyon Creek students, 9:30—depart for Seattle
Drivers, arrive by 9:00—check in with office staff
Bring sack lunch or money to buy lunch at Seattle Center

Friday, December 17: Lunchtime performance for Northshore

Administration at Monte Villa administration building
Bring or wear concert attire—have it looking neat, please!
Eat early (recommend students bring a lunch to school)
Get ties and fobs, 11:45; get on busses at 12:00
Perform at Monte Villa around 12:35. Back by 1:30.

December 8, 7:00 P.M.: Skyview Music Department Concert (optional)

Skyview Gymnasium (all bands, choruses and orchestra)

Marimba Ensemble

Requirements for participation:

- Must be a sixth grader
- Must be able to attend rehearsals—after school until 4:20, Monday and Friday
- Must have parent and teacher support
- Must have strong attendance record at school
- Must be willing to independently practice—minimum 1 lunch recess per week
- Must be a team player
- Must be able to participate in performances (May/June)
- Must show desire to improve (in skill, ability)
- Must show the ability to listen, wait and maintain focus
- Must be patient and supportive of others
- Must realize that 99% of all decisions will be made by Mrs. Bourne
- Must show evidence of being trustworthy, in all places—school and home
- Must submit completed application before consideration

Qualifications for entry and continued membership:

- Attendance at rehearsals—two unexcused absences results in dismissal
- All paperwork, letters, permission slips, etc. kept track of and turned in on time
- Evidence of lunch recess attendance and practice
- Outward support of others, patience in rehearsal, knowing when to play
- Contributing to the group (instrument maintenance, helpful attitude)
- Timely arrival at rehearsal, especially for after school patrol/bus personnel
- Timely departure after rehearsal (parent pick-up or other)

Schedule of events:

January 20:   Parent and teacher contracts distributed to all sixth graders eligible for participation

January 31:   Submit completed application to Mrs. Bourne (it won't help to give it to your classroom teacher—it is the applicant's responsibility to turn it in)

February 15: Roster of marimba ensemble members posted (limited to 20–24; included in the list will be alternates)

March 3:   First after-school rehearsal

A Day in Pike Street Market

A music program presented by the third- and fourth-grade students at Canyon Creek. Directed by Mrs. Bourne.

Parent information

When is it?

Tuesday, April 4th. Daytime performance at 9:45. Evening performance at 7:00.

Where?

Both performances will be in the Canyon Creek gym.

How are students involved?

In every way possible! Each student has a special responsibility. Every effort should be made to be sure they attend both performances.

Will my student need to stay after school for rehearsals?

For the most part, no. However, there are several students who will help design, build and paint the backdrops and stage setting. They know who they are—they will receive a permission slip to remain at school for Tuesday, March 28 or Wednesday, March 29.

How can parents help?

In many ways! We would like to have props representing what you might find in a Pike Street shop, especially the following: fake fruit or fake baked goods, fake flowers, inexpensive paintings, Australian goods, African artifacts, anything from the Caribbean (posters, especially); a boy's or men's suit coat and dress pants (to hang up, not to wear); something one might wear as formal wear in Korea or Norway; and Native American jewelry or artifacts. If your son/daughter will help with the set design, we could use adult help at that time, as well. Please e-mail me for details. All props should be to Mrs. Bourne by March 24, if possible.

What's the program about?

Some typical students spend a day in Pike Street market, discovering the many nationalities found there—each has a story and a song that reflects their culture.

Anything else?

Be sure to write the date in your calendars and notify coaches and others of that evening's commitment at school.

The 2006 Annual Sixth-Grade Variety Show

Ways to Be Involved:

1. Performer

All types of 'acts' possible—think entertainment

2. Equipment mover

Helps move all necessary equipment before, during and after the show

3. Sound equipment

Helps run the sound system, manages the microphones, mic stands, runs CDs as needed, etc.

4. Promotion

Writes 'blurbs' for the *Coyote Crier* and the *Howler;* must be able to work within a deadline

5. Decorations

Decides what kinds of decorations would make the gym and gym stage unique, since this show is unique

6. Introductions and Masters of Ceremony

Announces performers

7. Lighting effects

Runs spotlights, turns lights on and off from side of gym and from behind the stage

8. Program distribution

Hands out the program to all adults entering the gym for the show

9. "Gopher"

Is sure all people involved in an upcoming act are by the stage, ready to go on

10. Guiding committee

Serves as a class representative, attending planning meetings during two lunch recesses, posts sign-up sheets and informational bulletins in classrooms

Performance Expectations

Primary Grades

1. Keep your hands to yourself

2. Stay in your space

3. Sing the correct words to the songs

4. Show the song in your face and eyes

5. If you need help with words, look at Mrs. Bourne

6. Keep silent after a song is over and smile at the audience!

7. When people say "that was really great!," smile and say, "Thanks—glad you enjoyed it!"

8. If you are playing an instrument, keep it silent until it's time to play your part.

9. Remember that you are entertaining with a whole big group. It's the music and what the group is doing that counts.

10. Think of someone you want to honor with your behavior, your musicianship and your focus on the performance.

Yep, It's Time!

Big week for the chorus:

Tuesday

Chorus members

Arrive at Bothell High School by 5:45. (Someone will be on the look-out for students, and will direct them to where they need to be)

Parents

- Take desserts to the library (someone will be available to direct you there)
- Doors to the concert hall will open at 6:35
- *Tie and fob helpers*—Please come back stage when doors open (around 6:35) to help
- The Bothell High School Jazz Choir and Women's Choir will be our special guests, and will perform during the first half of the concert. You don't want to miss these two fantastic groups.
- With 600 seats, there's room for many!

Thursday

- Wear concert attire to school
- Warm-up in music room, 8:45
- Chaperones, please arrive by 8:50
- School assembly, 9:00
- Depart for Seattle, 10:00
- Lunch—either bring $ or a sack lunch; eat real food that's real good for you!
- Bank of America Tower, 12:00 concert

PERFORMANCE THIS WEEK!

Chorus Members,

Performance is on Thursday, March 13, at Northshore Baptist Church. Take a left on Juanita, also called 100th Street (off Bothell Way, across from the Yakima Fruit Market). Head south, as if going to Kirkland. Turn left on NE 145th. The church is on the south side of the street, very near the corner of Juanita/100th and 145th.

Please plan to arrive by 6:15 P.M. to adequately warm-up, get ties/fobs, etc. We will have a room to meet in—come in the main entrance and look for someone to direct you. The concert begins at 7:00 P.M.

Wear your full chorus attire. (I do have a few boys' shirts at school, if needed/desired.)

Mrs. Bourne

Timeline for 1st/2nd-grade program, April 5
Prepared for Instructional Staff

Month of January and Early February
Introduce music, dances, instrumental parts, storyline
Get schedule and info to teachers/Meg
Reserve the gym

February 3–10
Distribute list of responsibilities for students to prioritize and select

February 14–18
Inform students of their 'extras'
Get job list to teachers
Distribute scripts to speakers
Order additional chairs

Remainder of February/Early March
Finish teaching songs to all in class
Speakers and other special performers meet for recess practices
Assessment based on song literature (rhythm, pitch, form, dynamics)

Week of March 7
Continue practice with speakers
Meet with students who want to help build the sets
Begin sketching scenery and props needed
Send letter to parents—information and volunteers

Week of March 14
Props, sets, costumes coming together
Stay after school at least one day to help do some painting

Week of March 21
Make sure artwork and designs for gym are ready
Begin grouping music classes together

Week of March 28
Programs sent to Graphics Center
Group rehearsals, with run-throughs in the gym by week's end

Week of April 4
Final run-through
Assembly performance—1:30–2:00, Tuesday
Evening performance—children come around 6:40; program starts at 7:00

Finding 'It' and Staying in the Music Classroom

It's been a match made in heaven. That's how I've felt about every school that's hired me as music teacher. I've been fortunate: time, freedom, access, good luck, and great circumstances have allowed me to find the right place to teach at the right time. Although my experiences have been geographically varied, each and every setting has been a wonderful fit. What made each place professionally gratifying? Writing this text has provided an excellent opportunity to reflect on the many employment choices made over the course of several years. Each decision was spurred by a variety of parameters that helped provide a path toward the place. In this final chapter, consideration of these parameters, or variables, for finding, securing and extending employment as a music educator are included.

Finding the right place at the right time is one thing; getting hired is another. It requires a successful meeting between those who are hiring and the job seeker. The interview helps both employer and employee discover whether it's a match. If it is and a contract is offered, what can the new teacher expect from school administrators and what will they expect of him or her? How can one best develop a professional and productive relationship with colleagues and administrators? When a principal observes a music teacher, what is considered and evaluated?

Finally, staying in the classroom requires continued professional development, as well as a successful period of non-tenured status. Although the legislative rules differ from state to state, there are common experiences that most music teachers find effective and helpful for professional growth options.

Finding *the* place, preparing for and passing the interview, signing the contract, meeting the administrator's and colleague's expectations of effectiveness, and continuing professional growth are realities of this wonderful profession. When the match is made, the career begins. Welcome to the search.

Finding *the* Place: Common Variables

Once the degree was completed, my job search began and has been repeated five times as 26 years passed. In all cases, there were common parameters used to help guide my decisions. Looking back on the choices I made for school settings, finding the fit was a combination of five variables:

1. The adults who represented the school and/or district had personalities, philosophies and outlooks on instruction that aligned with my personality, philosophy and instructional perspective.
2. The location suited my family's particular needs and circumstances, as well as my own.
3. The culture and community fit the kind of population I was interested in living with and working for.
4. The school and/or district were committed to supporting music education for their students.
5. The timing was right. I was ready for a change, and a particular place was looking for someone like me.

All of these factors have influenced the employment decisions I've made. They may have little to no impact for other job seekers, but they've more than proven their effectiveness for me.

Let's consider each variable individually:

1. People and Personality

In previous chapters, I've described instances of the support I received during those first crucial years: I've not emphasized, however, the impact *continued* support has made. Regardless of experience and 'veteran teacher' status, surrounding oneself with adults who supply encouragement fuels the desire to recharge one's battery for improved instruction year after year. One looks forward to being among people who seek the best for you.

Teaching is not an isolated career—far from it! It functions at a more powerful level when conceived of as a community of professionals who support each other and share ideals of service for students. When looking for a teaching position, the attraction to be employed one place or another *must* include the human factor. New teachers, as well as veterans, profit from being around those who invite collaborative input and creative energy.

Effective educators rely on colleagues to provide advice, friendship, ideas, and inspiration. When educators are encircled with professionals who believe in them, the net results yield not only success but also a sense of belonging. Speaking from personal experience, I know how critical belonging is when the first job is in an unfamiliar place and far from one's family.

As described in Chapter 2, human beings have a basic need to belong. Teachers are no different. In truth, music teachers at the elementary level normally belong to every student and staff member in the building. Their influence and effect in the school as a whole is far reaching, as the music teacher establishes professional connections with all instructional staff and students.

When a music teacher is embraced as part of an educational team, community develops and healthy relationships result. Courage and confidence grow. When a support network exists, the educator is encouraged to stretch professionally. I probably would not have pursued the leadership positions I've been privileged to experience had collegial support not been apparent.

In each of the interviews that led to employment, I felt some human connection with those that met with me at the school location. Something communicated, "These are people you want to have around you at this time in your professional life." There was a common philosophy of living and learning, a similar sense of mission, and an obvious integrity and respect for the profession. There was a feeling of adventure and forward thinking. In short, the adults I wanted to work with had qualities I'd normally look for in a friend.

One's personality naturally filters who he or she likes being around. Since quality educational systems have teaching staffs that function collaboratively, it makes sense to find a place where one's point of view is expected, respected and welcomed. This is certainly easier when a general comfort level is felt and personalities gel with others in the building. I've genuinely liked the people at my schools and have felt they genuinely liked me.

Strong indicates, "The teacher's personality is one of the first sets of characteristics to look for in an effective teacher.

Many aspects of effective teaching can be cultivated, but it is difficult to effect change in an individual's personality."[1] (This quote returns us to "Who Are You?" in Chapter 1.)

Schools have a personality, as well. Although personnel may fluctuate, the overall persona of the school—the impression it makes beyond the building walls—will often remain consistent, barring unforeseen events. Consideration of the school's personality is important, as it reflects on all of the educators associated with it. For this reason, it's important that prospective music teachers interview in the actual school building if at all possible.

I've known recent graduates who have accepted positions without a face-to-face encounter with the adults they'd be working with. While I admire their bravery, I know a critical part of my professional happiness is attributed to those I've chosen to work around. Therefore, before accepting a new position as a music teacher, I strongly suggest one consider the following:

- Does my personality—who I am—match what they want?
- Do I believe the personality of the school (or district) fits what I'm looking for?
- Are the people I know from the school (or district) the kind of people I'd normally seek out in a professional relationship?
- Does the school (or district) project an image I'm comfortable with?
- Do I sense an atmosphere of mutual trust and respect?
- Will this administrator and the school's classroom teachers welcome my opinion?
- Will I be accepted for who I am and will I feel proud to be associated with the adults in this school (or district)?

2. Location

While the people one chooses to teach with are clearly driven by personality preferences, the location is often determined by circumstance. When I graduated from college, I was single, interested in living somewhere 'different', and was stable emotionally and financially. Moving was very possible and very attractive to me—it was a decision I made freely and one that I do not regret.

---

[1] Stronge, 78.

Not many people have the advantages, circumstances or the desires I had for relocating. One of the music teachers I recently mentored sought employment in her hometown. She needed (and wanted) to live with family, desired the support of familiar people, and was drawn to the location by a thorough knowledge of the area. Our circumstances differed, yet my first year and her first year were successful in all respects. I was satisfied with the change of scenery while she was satisfied with the familiarity.

By choosing to move, the range of job possibilities was expansive for me. I was interested in living anywhere west of the Mississippi and sent countless letters of interest to places that sounded intriguing. In the case of my mentee, the areas she investigated were far more limited. Fortunately for both us, a match was found in the locations we desired: I ended up in Oklahoma, and she ended up at home. We both won.

3. Culture and Community

The culture and community of an area defines a set of beliefs, practices and perspectives a group of people tend to share. They can be defined by setting (rural vs. urban vs. suburban), by the socioeconomic base (low-income vs. upper-class), or by the nationality of the people found in that particular area. New teachers are wise to carefully consider the kind and type of community and culture that attracts them to a particular area.

Recently, I met a music educator pursuing a master's degree. Her first experience with teaching was located in the

housing project area of Chicago. This culture was unfamiliar to her, having been raised in the upper-middle-class sections of Seattle. She chose to move into this area, intrigued by the possibilities and challenges it would offer. I admired her confidence and conviction.

It was not curiosity that fueled her interest in this particular culture; rather, it was her desire to experience cultures different than her own. In fact, once the master's degree was completed, she searched for and was hired on a Native American reservation, ready to begin yet another adventure.

Obviously, new and different people interested and intrigued her, personally and professionally. Whether in the low-income areas of Chicago or on the reservation, this music educator was able to view her students as 'just kids'. According to her, they included students who wanted to learn and those who "didn't know yet that they wanted to learn." It sounds like her students are like others one would find in many communities!

A supportive community has always been appealing to me. When I've considered a school, district or area, I've tried to learn as much as I can about the community prior to the interview. This process is increasingly easier to do now than it used to be, as the internet offers every bit of data one might be interested in knowing and more. There's really no excuse to not be fully informed.

4. Evidence of Supporting Music Education and Overall Reputation

After I married and had a family, this parameter became increasingly important. I did not want to move our family only to learn my position would be cut after one year. Security and potential longevity in a position was a strong variable to consider. In addition, my husband and I wanted to live and pay taxes in an area where educational dollars were well spent and a balanced curriculum was available for our children.

One particular teaching position became available while I was teaching at the university level. I was interested in providing authentic instructional opportunities for our undergraduates, and this school was looking for affordable ways to offer elementary music to their K–5 students. The people I knew and met at the school were excited to start, the location suited our family, and there was more than enough evidence to indicate the community wanted their children to have music class.

Teaching at this school two days a week was enveloped into my university schedule and provided extraordinary experiences for our music education majors and for me. Due to the positive response offered by the staff, parents and students (university and elementary level), the position eventually became full time. I was tremendously proud of the school and its community for the steps they made to improve the overall quality of education for their children.

My current district has a long and distinguished reputation for supporting music education. Within two months of arriving in Washington (in 1985), I'd learned of the districts that attracted and maintained quality music educators. In addition, each elementary school in the district had a full time music educator (a situation that is not as common as it should be). When the time came to move from my university post to a public school position, the choice of location and community was easily decided.

5. Timing

I've always felt my timing has been right-on. Call it luck, call it circumstances, or call it meant to be, when I was ready for a new teaching position, a particular educational setting was ready for me. At one point, I was invited to accept a position I'd interviewed for, but the timing wasn't right and I declined. This proved to be a wise move, since the principal who interviewed me was not the one I'd be working with. Personnel changed dramatically and I would have walked into a building with little carry-over from the previous spring when I interviewed.

Timing not only works for being hired, but it's also an indicator of when one should graciously leave. There have been times one teacher or another has changed positions, left to pursue a graduate program, or shifted from one school to another. When asked "Why now?" the answer is almost always, "Well, the timing seemed right." When it's time to leave one location for another, every attempt should be made to provide the new teacher with the space and freedom to establish a new era. One can only hope the prior teacher would do the same in one's new location.

While going to a new place was easy, leaving wasn't. The relationships I formed extended beyond those of a job. Saying goodbye to students and colleagues was the most challenging issue I have faced in moving from one school to the next; I can truly say I left my heart in many locations.

My career as a music teacher can be tracked by its timing: four years in Oklahoma, two years in Arizona, ten years in Central Washington, eleven years in Western Washington. Every move was accompanied with a touch of sadness but a realization that it was the right time to leave. No regrets, as it has always been for the best. Just lucky? Maybe. But somehow, I've definitely been fortunate.

Finding 'the' place to begin, continue or end one's career is a process not to be approached lightly. Taking the time to apply parameters for choosing the right position at the right time can make all the difference in how one perceives teaching as a career. The right place can lift, hold and inspire. The wrong place? I'm grateful to have not experienced that.

Interviewing

Once the decision is made to apply for a teaching position, the wait begins. "Will I get called for an interview?" "Will my application and résumé draw someone's attention?" "Should I call someone or just be patient?" "I wonder how I stack up against the other candidates for this job?" Doubting questions bombard most new graduates. However, once the invitation is made to actually interview, the real questioning begins.

My first interview was in Oklahoma at a school where the music teaching position was conceived as pivotal to every staff member. Therefore, *every* staff member volunteered to come to my initial interview. It was held at 7:00 A.M. on a school day.

I was asked to meet the interview 'team' in the staff room. When I entered, approximately 40 faces greeted me. Surprise! My university professors had wished me luck and coached me on possible questions, but no one ever predicted 40 people (including the custodian of the school) would be inclined to show up.

Once the initial interview concluded, I was asked to meet some of the children in the school. In groups of three or four, kids greeted me in the library and asked their questions while I was observed from afar by different staff members. It was easy to tell relationships between teachers and students were valued. They wanted to be sure a genuine comfort level existed between the music-teacher candidate and the children.

In the late afternoon, I met with two administrators at the district office, and by that evening, I was invited to accept the position. Twelve hours had passed since my initial meeting with the staff. Something had clicked with them and with me. I knew this was the right school in the right place. I accepted the job without hesitation. Why? 1. It was clear to me that this school valued people. They believed in the potential of each learner, child or adult. They also believed in the value of the teacher-student relationship. 2. The interview questions revealed how integral and dynamic music was in their school. Kids didn't 'go to music' for 35 minutes twice a week; it was considered an integral part of their total education. 3. The school building, its grounds and the surrounding community were inviting. I felt comfortable among the population, culture and location. It was the right place to be at that time in my life, and I knew it.

Over time, I've shared my first-interview story with many music educators. So far, no one has experienced anything quite like I did. It was a one-time-only event I'll always remember, not only due to the unusual size of the interview team but also for the extreme value placed on the music position.

In most elementary music interviews, candidates meet with the building principal, classroom teachers from primary and intermediate grades, and maybe a specialist in the building (PE or Library, usually). The team normally asks questions that provide them with a sense of who the candidate is and how effectively that individual functions in a school setting. They are searching for someone who can effectively teach and seamlessly fit their collaborative team of teachers.

Stronge indicated that educators display certain characteristics. These behaviors fit into five categories and are closely linked to those qualities sought in candidates for teaching positions:

1. Who the teacher is as a person
2. Classroom management and system
3. Organizing and sequencing instruction
4. Monitoring student progress and potential
5. Professional demeanor[2]

Each of these characteristics was included in comments made by three individuals I recently met with. I asked an elementary principal, a district music coordinator and a second-year teacher (who successfully interviewed for a position in a new district) to describe their interview processes and/or experiences. Each offered unique perspectives as to techniques and criteria used for seeking employees, or to become employed.

The principal I talked with believes all positions in her school are instructionally based, regardless of academic area or grade level. Therefore, she and the interview team in her building frame their screening and interview process based on the desire to find a "good quality instructor." In order to find the right person, they ask the candidate to comment on the following:

- Introduce who he is, personally, as well as describe professional experiences
- Describe his beliefs about teaching and the school as 'community'
- Discuss music pedagogically, e.g. the developmental sequence of music instruction (difference between a first-grade and sixth-grade lesson, for instance)
- Describe how he views himself as a learner
- Articulate beliefs on issues such as integration, involvement with a team of instructors, awareness of role in the school, etc.

This principal is interested in finding teachers who believe in effective, high-standard instruction, can contribute as a col-

---

[2] *Ibid.*, 77.

league, and will design and implement age-appropriate lessons. In addition, the music educator she and her team are looking for should show evidence of a commitment to students and acknowledge a desire to continue learning and molding the craft. As new teachers, particularly, "Their learning has only begun."[3] The disposition to pursue professional-growth opportunities is a quality effective educators display throughout their careers.

The interview team at this principal's school includes herself, classroom teachers (usually one primary, one intermediate), another specialist, and, ideally, parents. When asked whether she would interview someone for a music position on her own, she said, "No. That position is too valuable to an entire school culture. If a team is not in place, I would call members of my staff until I had a balanced group to conduct the interview."

From another perspective, the district coordinator I met with asks music teacher candidates how "committed they are to making music teaching a career," in whatever position they are applying for. As music coordinator, he serves as a member of several interview teams, particularly at the secondary level. Candidates for junior high positions who indicate "they really want to teach high school" send up a red flag to him. "I want to know they are committed to teaching the particular age they're interviewing to work with and are not using it as a 'stepping stone' for an alternative setting."[4]

When interviewing candidates, this district coordinator looks for signs of "passion, excitement and enthusiasm" from potential teachers. "I want our district filled with the best people I can find for our students."

A teacher I formally mentored recently completed her second year as an elementary music teacher in our district. Admittance to medical school for her husband necessitated a move. Once the new location was known, this ambitious music educator got to work. She researched the districts nearby, visited Web sites, and talked with veteran teachers about their perceptions of the school districts near their location. Applications and résumés were sent, and interview requests soon followed.

I met with her a week after she'd accepted a position in a very fine district near their new address. Her interview team included four music educators (two from the elementary level,

---

[3] Angela Kerr, interview by author, Bothell, WA, 2006.
[4] Ted Christensen, interview by author, Bothell, WA, 2006.

one from secondary and the district music coordinator). No building principals, no classroom teachers, just representatives of the district who were given the task of selecting music teachers for openings in their area.

Among the many questions asked, one request from the team stood out to her more than others: They wanted to see a three-minute lesson on rhythm. It could be for any grade level, as long as she informed them ahead of time. A few members of the team volunteered to serve as students while others observed. During our time together, she reported that this particular part of the interview was unusual, but fun, resulting in the two elementary music teachers jotting down the content and song taught. They indicated, "Never pass up a chance to get a great lesson idea." Quite a compliment for any music teacher to hear, particularly a relatively new teacher!

For every job, there are a myriad of unique interview techniques employed. When I taught at the university, some of our adventurous graduates applied for positions in remote villages in Alaska with phone-only interviews. A few faced screening committees (in larger districts) that asked candidate after candidate the same general questions in order to discern which teachers would progress to the next level of interview. Finally, some were hired two days before school began, with a somewhat-frantic principal making last-minute contacts.

Regardless of conditions or techniques used, I do suggest that the candidate pose questions at the interview. The more information one gathers, the better informed the decision. In addition to gaining more information, the interview team will interpret the questions asked as an indication of interest and thoughtfulness. MENC: The National Association of Music Education hosts a very informative section on their Web site called "A Career Guide to Music Education."[5] Included are well over 100 possible interview questions, templates for cover letters, outlines for résumés, as well as questions candidates might ask of the interviewers.

If the school and potential teacher are a match, the candidate and interview team consider working together as an attractive and positive proposition. However, if the candidate falls short of convincing the interviewer he or she is the individual they are looking for, invitations will not follow.

---

[5] The address for this web page is www.menc.org/industry/job/career.html.

I strongly urge candidates to consider their strengths and weaknesses—as people, as teachers and as colleagues—prior to entering the interview setting. Most teacher applicants are asked to speak of their positive qualities, as well as those they wish to improve. Learning how to articulate both, without bragging or self-destructing, is crucial. I've known some excellent music education graduates who have faced unemployment over this simple, yet vital, skill. They felt too boastful to speak highly of themselves and were inclined to emphasize their weaknesses in ways that were interpreted as self-defeating. I believe it is possible to speak the truth about oneself and maintain an air of confidence, but it takes practice.

My own experience as part of an interview team has been varied. Regardless of the teaching position being sought, I've always found myself attracted to candidates who seem real. I enjoy meeting educators who know who they are, like who they are, and know that they have much to offer students. I'm struck by their personalities first, and all other qualities second.

Students learn from teachers who like being in the presence of others. They are motivated to learn from individuals who believe in children as capable people. They are attracted to educators who are positive, who want to be in their role as teacher, and who are able to structure the classroom so that learning can blossom. Interview teams want to know a music teacher has the capacity to do these things; it's the candidate's job to communicate in a manner such that the match, if it is to be made, is obvious.

Administrators and First-Year Expectations

Throughout my career, I've relied on my building and district administrators for professional leadership, insight, empathy, and honesty. I've asked for help in developing perspective, settling a problem, or solving a dilemma. At times, my administrators offered advice but left final decisions and solutions in my lap. Sometimes, an administrator prevented me from acting in ways I might later regret.

The educational settings I've been drawn to had administrators who inspired, supported and encouraged me to keep my sights on quality instruction. They instilled confidence in my skills as teacher and in my sense of well being as a person. Each exceeded what anyone might expect from a boss.

What should a new music teacher expect from his or her building administrator? What do most principals expect from their new teachers? I've served as music educator with nine different building administrators. Each contributed to my professional growth, some more abundantly than others, but all positively.

One of my principals came into the music classroom at least once each week. She would stand in the back of the room and watch or sit right down with the kids. Often, she left a short note positioned on my computer keyboard. The content of those short notes always brightened my day. I still have most of them in my school drawer.

I began to expect to see her each week and learned to rely on her impressions of my improvement and progress as an educator. Since she observed me so often, the formal observation evaluations proved an extension of those shorter, casual drop-in visits.

While new teachers shouldn't necessarily expect weekly visits from their principals, there are a few traits I've found evident with the building administrators I've met or worked for. In my experience, effective administrators tend to:

- Define their role as the leader or facilitator of the school
- Maintain an open-door policy
- Invite input, encourage collaboration, and welcome points of view from all staff members—even the new ones
- Be visible in the classroom, at concerts, at assemblies, and at school events
- Provide structures for success, especially for new staff members (partnering them with a school mentor, providing a tour of the building, introducing them to the entire staff, etc.)

From my perspective, the role of the building principal is overwhelming and under appreciated. Principals have an unending list of must do's, yet most take the time to let their teachers vent, brag, cry, complain, boast, and question. I have done each of these with most of the nine principals I've worked with, and they still remained steadfast supporters.

I admit it. I've been spoiled to expect certain qualities from my superiors. I know I've received extraordinary attention and encouragement and am not sure whether my opinion and experience alone provides the real story of what a new teacher should or might expect. Perhaps, if nothing else, it shows a glimpse of what could be.

In order to provide a different perspective, I talked with a building principal with whom I've not served. This principal admits to having very little musical experience, yet must observe, coach and provide instructional assistance to the music educator in her building. When I asked what a music teacher could expect from her, she answered, "That I will be there to support him; I don't want a new teacher to feel embarrassed to come to me if they have a problem. I'm not necessarily going to solve the problem, but I'll help the teacher retrace what he's done to confront the issue."[6]

This principal indicated that new teachers should expect to see her in the classroom as casual observer, as evaluator and as admirer. "Sometimes, I get involved and will ask the students to tell me about their activity. This is especially helpful when I might not understand the terminology being used in the music class."

Beyond classroom involvement, Ms. Kerr expects new teachers to be involved as a contributing staff member. "A school can't run by everybody just doing their job—teachers need to step beyond their classrooms and be open to the view of others."

Individuals are hired as teachers for their perceived effectiveness in the classroom *and* as members of a collaborative staff. "There should be a 'comfort level' evident, as well as a confidence, in being involved and included." The music teacher, in particular, is wrapped within the culture and community of a given school and should feel comfortable filling that particular role.

Beyond casually dropping in to watch, formal observations exist in all facets of education. The first evaluation can feel a bit like one's first recital; it certainly follows some of the protocol:

- Practice and preparation are evident from the performer (the teacher). A written guide (lesson plan) informs the audience (the principal) of the repertoire (concepts, skills, materials) to be observed.
- The variety and excellence of the program engages everyone in the concert hall (classroom).
- Thunderous applause (the post-observation meeting) follows.

---

[6] Kerr, 2006.

In a formal observation, the principal is anxious to learn how the music educator organizes and presents information in a way that meets educational standards. This process can be explained during the pre-observation conference. However, the actual observation in the classroom provides the other piece: What is the 'feeling tone' like? How do the children respond? What level of thinking, questioning and interacting occurs?

After the first couple of formal observations, I began to look forward to them. They provided a means for the students to display their skills in front of a critical 'audience member' and provided me with a glimpse of how I was progressing as a teacher. I still look forward to them after 26 years. Formal observations represent, in a sequential and predictable manner, what I can expect from my principal and what he or she can continue to expect from me.

Recently, I looked through a scrapbook from my teaching days in Oklahoma. Included in the scrapbook were documentations of the written evaluations I received after my first two formal observations. They were surrounded by the many notes and cards of encouragement received from my principal. One particular note demonstrates the quality and level of personal and professional support I was given that first year:

Dear Patty,

I thought I'd write you a serious note. I tease so constantly. I do have a great deal of confidence in you—but not in a 'product' I expect—just confidence in you. I'm certain you must be overwhelmed. I was my first year. (Actually, I am each year!). Most of all what I want you to know is that all we expect is you to be you and to enjoy your profession.[7]

Fondly,
Judi

How can anyone fail with that kind of support?

Professional Development and Staying in the Music Class

Effective teachers invest in their own education. They model to their students that education and learning are valuable by taking classes and participating in professional development, conferences, and in-service training. Effective teachers learn and grow as they expect their students to learn and grow.[8]

Progressing from novice to mastery level in teaching requires more than time in the classroom. Real progress is made when educators meet with others, read professional literature, develop new skills, and expand their repertoire of teaching

---

[7] Written by Dr. Judi Ford Barber. Used by permission.
[8] Stronge, 20.

techniques. While the first year can be overwhelming in multiple ways, it is just the beginning of a teacher's education.

In a recent discussion with a district music coordinator on the topic of professional growth and development, the following suggestions were offered, particularly for new teachers:

- Connect with seasoned professionals who can offer perspective, wisdom, advice, and resources for use in the music classroom
- Attend professional conferences. Each state has a MENC affiliate hosting a state or regional conference; in addition, there are opportunities to become involved in specialized areas of music (Orff, Kodály, Dalcroze, etc.) during weekend workshops. Publishers of Basel and choral series, retail music stores and music publishers also host workshops that provide excellent materials and opportunities to view new products.
- Develop relationships and pathways with colleagues; they often have suggestions for particular references and resources one might investigate to learn more about a particular topic or area in education—not necessarily in music

A music educator was recently interviewed for an elementary position in our district and was asked if she had any questions of the interview team. Her first question? "What kind of professional development opportunities are provided for the teachers of this district?" She was hired.

While the 'right' question won't necessarily get the job, the right attitude will. The disposition to recognize the value and importance of continuing education indicates the commitment one feels toward his or her profession. It is a way of life for the effective educator.

Most states require some degree of continuing education for advanced certification. This information is available through a state's Department of Education. Regardless of requirement, teachers who plan to stay in the music classroom for a career continually find ways to improve their craft.

I'll close this chapter with an email I recently received from a first-year music teacher. This young educator interned in my building not long ago. Her communiqué reflects the enthusiasm and joy one can expect to reap when teaching in the *right* place with the *right* people at the *right* time:

> Tuesday was the 2nd/3rd-grade program. It went really well. The whole gym was packed and the kids were so happy. They were singing their hearts out. [This school] is mostly low-income, and the population is very [diverse], so to see all of those parents there was awesome! The next day, my principal observed me with a 6th-grade class. We were working on xylophones, learning tunes from Walt Hampton's *Hot Marimba* book. They absolutely love it. The observation went great! I had my meeting with her yesterday and she had nothing but good things to say! That was a relief! The great thing was I wasn't nervous when she was in my room. I think my confidence has grown a lot this year. We also talked about next year. Things are looking good![9]

---

[9] Written by Carly Ferguson. Used by permission.

Final Thoughts

Music teaching is an extraordinary profession. Multiple levels of know-how go into doing the job well. However, when one looks at what an effective teacher knows, believes, practices, and implements, the core of music teaching is really quite simple! It is based on two basic premises and abilities:

- The ability to inspire
- The ability to see the positive

Throughout this book, lists of questions, time frames and tips are offered for consideration. Each list links back to these two simple things. Before ending this text, I offer a few more thoughts to consider as preparation for going into the music class.

The List

I'm a list maker, with spiral notebooks full of ideas to try, contacts to make, books to buy, CDs to listen to, and lesson possibilities galore. Over time, many 'remember' lists have been constructed. Inside my plan book is the following:

This year, I will remember...
- To keep an open mind and consider new ways of thinking and teaching.
- To protect my singing and speaking voice.
- When necessary, to chant the mantra, "I am the adult in this situation."
- That repetition and small steps are good.

- That productive behavior can be taught.
- That anticipation is a good thing. Allow children to look forward to events. Don't rush them.
- To be more organized so that optimal learning happens, even when I'm absent.
- To not be afraid of conflict; it will happen.
- That being mean feels terrible afterwards. There's never a reason to be mean.
- That fatigue is an enemy—it makes me the kind of person most people do not want to be around.
- To bend, flex, breathe, and question before jumping to conclusions or jumping down someone's throat.
- To observe the kids in alternate settings.
- To not let bad days and mistakes cause feelings of personal failure.
- To ask colleagues how their day is going.